Christmas 2001

with love to Pete

from

Val

Best Sermons Ever

Best Sermons Ever

Edited by

Christopher Howse

CONTINUUM

London and New York

Continuum

The Tower Building, 11 York Road, London SE1 7NX
370 Lexington Avenue, New York NY 10017-6503

© Continuum International Publishing 2001

Text © Christopher Howse

British Library Cataloguing-in-Publication Data
A catalogue record for this book is available from the British Library.

ISBN 0-8264-5685-5

Every effort has been made to trace the copyright holders of original
material contained in this volume. The author and publishers would be
interested to hear from any copyright holders we have been unable to
contact, so that full acknowledgement may be made in future editions.

Typeset by Kenneth Burnley in Wirral, Cheshire.
Printed and bound in Great Britain by Biddles Ltd,
Guildford and King's Lynn.

Contents

Introduction   ix

Sermon One: *Peter the Apostle*   1
   The end in view (St Ignatius)   3

Sermon Two: *John Chrysostom*   5
   Prayer for the Virgin's intercession, fourth century   10
   Extract from an ancient homily for Holy Saturday:
      Christ's descent into the underworld   11
   God's protection (St Patrick)   13

Sermon Three: *St Augustine*   15
   Night prayer (Alcuin)   18

Sermon Four: *Aelfric*   19
   Watch over me (St Dunstan)   26

Sermon Five: *St Bernard*   27
   Come, Creator Spirit   31
   Sermon notes by Thomas Aquinas for the feast of
      St Bartholomew the Apostle   31
   Prayer of giving (St Francis of Assisi)   34
   Private devotions   35

Sermon Six: *The Homilies* 37
  Patience works (St Teresa of Avila) 43

Sermon Seven: *Lancelot Andrewes* 45
  Morning prayer (Lancelot Andrewes) 57

Sermon Eight: *John Donne* 59
  The call (George Herbert) 78

Sermon Nine: *Jeremy Taylor* 79
  Prayer (Book of Common Prayer) 86

Sermon Ten: *John Bunyan* 87
  Help for prisoners: Prayer after sentence of death
    (John Gother) 95

Sermon Eleven: *Jonathan Swift* 97
  Melancholy (Christopher Smart) 106

Sermon Twelve: *Jonathan Edwards* 109
  A prayer found in Mrs Chapone's handwriting after
    her death (Hester Chapone) 125

Sermon Thirteen: *John Wesley* 127
  A prayer that may be daily said by a woman in the
    state of pregnancy (Richard Challoner) 135

Sermon Fourteen: *Laurence Sterne* 137
  Hymn (Charles Wesley) 142

Sermon Fifteen: *Sydney Smith* 143
  Gunpowder treason (John Keble) 154

Sermon Sixteen: *John Henry Newman*   155
    The Blessed Sacrament (Gerard Manley Hopkins)   162

Sermon Seventeen: *Charles Spurgeon*   163
    Mary (Ronald Knox)   170

Sermon Eighteen: *Martin Luther King*   171
    Jesus (Mother Teresa)   177

Sermon Nineteen: *H. A. Williams*   179
    Extract from a sermon by Billy Graham, California, 1974   187
    Prayer for murderers (Bishop Dehqani-Tafti)   190

Sermon Twenty: *Pope John Paul II*   191

Sources and Further Reading   197

Introduction

People have listened to sermons eagerly and with pleasure for almost the whole span of the two millennia of Christianity. Our own age is the rare exception. There seems to be something wrong with present-day sermons. They are not just boring but embarrassing too. Yet there have been awkward times before. 'Preaching has become a by-word for long and dull conversation of any kind,' wrote Sydney Smith in the early nineteenth century, 'and whoever wishes to imply, in any piece of writing, the absence of everything agreeable and inviting calls it a sermon.'

To the best sermons, though, people have crowded. But what does 'best' mean? In this book are the twenty best sermons ever, plus extracts from more. It is a game of a sort to choose the twenty best. One criterion is literary. There is a book commonly found in secondhand shops called *The Bible Designed to be Read as Literature* (which of course it was not). For my money a sermon that might have been designed to be read as literature is the one by John Donne on the Holy Ghost printed here. Take his characterization of the sermon-hearer hungry for novelty, who is not 'satisfied with those Quailes which God sends, (the preaching of solid and fundamental doctrines) but must have birds of Paradise, un-revealed mysteries out of God's own bosome preached unto him'. Donne lived long enough ago for his use of language to be striking, but not so long ago as to make it obscure. He has point: 'Christ Jesus's way is to change water into wine; sorrow into joy: the Devil's way is to change wine into water.' He was a master of style, yes, but he had ideas, insights far above the verbal: 'All in all is from the love of God; but there is something for God to love.

There is a man, there is a soul in that man, there is a will in that soul; and God is in love with this man, and this soul, and this will, and would have it.' He has feeling: 'This indifference to accompany men of divers religions, in the acts of their religion, this multiplicity will end in a nullity, and we shall hew to ourselves Cisternes, broken Cisternes, that can hold no water. We shall scatter one religion into many, and those many shall vanish into none.' He can be practical: 'He upon whose hand-labour the sustentation of his family depends, may offend God in running after many working-dayes Sermons.' Donne's contemporary, Lancelot Andrewes, seems at first to attempt a merely verbal analysis of his text; it is only after a while that the reader realizes that he is saying something about faith quite as subtle as the penetrating twentieth-century philosopher G. E. M. Anscombe. By contrast, to read Donne *in extenso* (and that is why I wanted to print his sermon in its entirety) after sampling the bucket-chain of Lancelot Andrewes is like swimming in a strong sea, warm and clear. When one reads a sermon by him one thinks it the best ever, until one reads the next.

Donne became a Protestant; his sermons contain the doctrine he believed. Well, so do John Chrysostom's, from 1,200 years earlier. But what are we to make of his language, his style? It is utterly foreign. If we want to read it in English translation there is a double trap. If we use a high Victorian translation it sounds like a cross between the King James Version of the Bible and an exercise from Demosthenes. If, though, it is translated into current idiomatic speech, it sounds *more* modern than Donne, and strangely at odds with its reiterated figures of speech and archaic references to bowls of wine and runaway slaves. Some people have tried to mend much more recent sermons; there exists a book called *Sermons on Several Occasions by John Wesley translated into Modern English* by James D. Holway. But, to remedy Chrysostom, there is no answer; I have tried to steer a middle course by removing archaisms from a nineteenth-century translation.

It is slightly easier to know what a sermon is: it is an address delivered in church. Of course some were written and never delivered; some, like Wesley's and Bunyan's, were delivered outdoors. I have excluded non-Christian sermons. In another attempt at narrowing, or focusing, the book I have deliberately made this an Anglo-centric book. I mean that I have concentrated on sermons given by English speakers, but not excluded those who, like Augustine and Chrysostom and Bernard, had a solid place in the English-speaking tradition. Learned preachers, as many were, could and did read Augustine in his own fine Latin.

So there are no French sermons here, though Bossuet and Fénelon are glories of the French language. Nor are there Germans, though Luther cried out for inclusion. But if it is impossible to solve the problem of translation, we have with John Chrysostom's sermon printed here an extraordinary historical drama that catches the attention. The scene comes alive, with the deposed eunuch Eutropius cowering at the altar for sanctuary as the golden-mouthed bishop draws the lesson. Just as we think Chrysostom is in danger of being cruel, he rebukes the crowded cathedral for lack of a divine perspective to the humbled eminence grise in front of them.

Similarly it is for its dramatic historical impact that I include the sermon by Pope John Paul in his first visit to Poland after his election. Anyone who remembers the television pictures of hundreds of thousands of Poles applauding and chanting in support of their Pope will be old enough to understand why the downfall of Communism in Europe was so important and so unlooked-for. Pope John Paul made better sermons theologically – he brought a sharp intellect and deep spirituality to his office. But those early days in Poland were unrepeatable.

Go back 1,000 years, and alien assumptions and language are obvious in an Englishman like Aclfric. Anglo-Saxon culture was not crude or unsubtle, but Aelfric's sermon for the feast of St Edmund, the tale of a royal martyr's miracles, belongs to a technique of hagiography that we no longer care to accept. At the same time, it is not dreamlike, but full of hard realities: blood, thorns, wild beasts, golden reliquaries and the tool-bag of burglars.

Both hagiography and experiential reality seem to be absent from the mystic meditations of St Bernard. In expounding the Song of Solomon he was quite aware of the literal meaning of the text: the lover and the beloved, the bride and the groom. He is more bashful, though, about revealing his own inmost experience of God the Word than he is about the vigorous love poetry of the Old Testament writer.

Bernard was closer in time to the Book of Homilies of the sixteenth century than they are to us. But the rogationtide Homily printed here, on beating the bounds, belongs to a different world from Bernard's. Bernard countenanced a Crusade to vanquish error; the Homilies set out to make the godly best of the rural tradition of marking boundary stones. The Homilies belong to a reformed religion that would abominate Bernard's world on popes and monasteries, and even more his sacraments and mysteries. Yet the reformers of renaissance England were not closed to Bernard's spiritual world; he is quoted by King James's translators of the Bible, he was read by Cranmer, Hooker, Andrewes, Donne and the Caroline divines. But if the cowled figure of Bernard had shown itself in the streets of Elizabethan London, he would soon have been arraigned for heresy.

The centuries following the Reformation were harsh ones. The Princes who ruled nations absolutely almost presumed to keep the souls of their subjects. Cranmer, Archbishop of Canterbury, was burnt. Jeremy Taylor, after lying low during the English Civil Wars, was made a bishop in the northern part of Ireland, which had been subdued by the sword but remained almost completely hostile to him as an Anglican caught between Presbyterians deprived of their livings and Catholics who did not even share his language.

Just as we are prepared to accept the enthusiasm of the audience of St Augustine of Hippo, say, as they pressed forward in the hot North African gloom of a packed basilica, crying out in approval at the turns and tropes of a professional rhetorician, so we can understand that for people like Jeremy Taylor, Bunyan in prison or Teresa of Avila burning with divine love, a sermon might be a thing of very great interest indeed. But it was not enthusiasts alone that appreciated sermons in early modern Europe. As a worldling untroubled by the pangs of conscience, Samuel Pepys would be hard to equal. His times – in particular the years following the Restoration of the British monarchy in 1660, the decade he covered in his diary – were much like our own, with satisfaction in consumer durables, sharp competition in office life, a devotion to fashion, no great scruple in sexual affairs, and an uncritical acceptance of comedy and melodrama as long as they are novel. Pepys loved the theatre, but he enjoyed sermons too, always grading them in his diary on a scale of technical quality – not by the religious devotion that they might have evoked in him. 'A good, plain sermon', 'an excellent sermon' and so on. In 1668 he read (while being rowed down the Thames from London to Chatham) Abraham Wright's *Five Sermons in Five Several Styles*. Wright's intention, by juxtaposing sermons by Lancelot Andrewes and Joseph Hall beside parodies of the Nonconformist style, was to show the superiority of preachers of the Church of England. Pepys was not convinced: 'I do think, when all is done, that contrary to the design of the book, the Presbyterian style and the Independent are the best of the five for sermons to be preached in.' For all that, he habitually frequented Church of England churches, sometimes wandering from one to another on a Sunday, and he was glad to read the sermons of Jeremy Taylor, which he bought.

Although collections of sermons were bought – and read – it is not to be thought that all preachers read their sermons from manuscript in the pulpit. For preachers nervous of being able to remember all the sections of the sermon, the *ars memoriae* came to their aid. Different versions of the memory-man's art were popular throughout Europe from the renaissance to the mid-nineteenth century. Some books provided sets of verses that included mnemonics for the chief events of history. (In Newman's novel, *Loss and Gain*, published in 1848, the hero's little sister is expected to remember her classical history dates with the help of artificial memory.) In the seventeenth century, John

Aubrey tells the story of a preacher who used the trick of an imaginary *locus*, a place on which to pin the headings of his sermon. Some people imagined the rooms of a house for their *locus*; this preacher it seems used a lion, and was heard one day in the pulpit to say: 'And now I find I must finish, for I have reached the lion's tail.'

Not all congregations were keen to hear sermons. Aubrey also tells of a preacher at Oxford who knew it was time to wind up his sermon when he saw the proctors' men – the servants of the University officers – coming in wiping their beards, having, it was plain, nipped over to the alehouse for a pint or two in sermon time. Even among those who were in church, there could be resistance, as Hugh Latimer noted in 1549, when the state had decreed that printed homilies were to be read out in church. 'Though the priest read them never so well,' he complained, 'yet if the parish like them not, there is such talking and babbling in the church that nothing can be heard.'

Indifference, or competition, was more the problem in the eighteenth century. The narrator of the popular song 'Sally in our Ally' (by Henry Carey, who died in 1743) is an apprentice whose favourite day is Sunday, since he can then slope off in sermon time and meet his sweetheart Sally.

If in the eighteenth century the established Church of England was becoming, for some, dry as well as high (in the sense of an erastian, implicitly conservative body), it must be remembered that the period saw strong outbursts of emotion and even more extraordinary phenomena, associated chiefly with enthusiastic Nonconformist preachers. When Samuel Johnson spoke of a woman preaching resembling a dog walking on its hind legs, he was referring to a Quaker preacher. The early Quakers were associated, particularly in the prejudiced popular mind, with antinomianism, lack of due order, pretended miracles, messianism and, of course, the quaking, shaking, falling down and shrieking that gave this Society of Friends their nickname, Quakers. It is true that George Fox (1624–1691) believed his associates could perform miracles, and that the supporters of the early Quaker

James Nayler thought him something like the Messiah come again. But it was the preaching that regularly disturbed onlookers.

It was not just women preaching or speaking extempore that got the Quakers and other Nonconformists into trouble with the establishment. The Act of Uniformity of 1662, which appointed the Book of Common Prayer as the sole lawful liturgy in church, had also required preachers to be licensed. Local magistrates, especially during church time on a Sunday, could be harsh against hedge preachers with no licence from the bishop. This is what got John Bunyan into prison. He gives accounts of his refusal to be browbeaten by the justices in *Grace Abounding to the Chief of Sinners* and its sequels. One reason that we have little verbatim of Bunyan's preaching, is because his sermons had to be given where they could; another reason is that he spoke whatever his heart prompted. We do have from Bunyan's pen voluminous commentaries on Scripture, and these resemble the expository school of teaching that survives today, in which a text is followed closely, from clause to clause, and the preacher expounds the meaning, while provoking the heart to repentance, and an acceptance of Christ, salvation, the grace of God. Such sermons can lose a lot when written down.

The same sort of opprobrium that the Quakers, Independents, Presbyterians, Congregationalists and Baptists attracted in the late seventeenth century came the way of the Methodists in the succeeding century. The great convenience that saved John Wesley from the oppression of the law was that he was an ordained priest of the Church of England; even so, he was opposed by bishops and took to preaching in the open air or in meeting-houses. Methodism drew brickbats from the unsympathetic, both from the worldly and from the unbending wing of the Established Church. Tobias Smollett, in other ways a man of wide sympathies, expected to raise a laugh by getting the hero of his novel *Humphry Clinker* (1771) to join the Methodists.

Smollett as a Scotsman had been brought up in a country where Anglicanism was not the religion imposed by the state. The same circumstances applied in America. Methodism found a welcome in the New World where Puritans and Presbyterianism had thriven before. But since then there has grown up a literature of hostility to strict Nonconformity, Nathaniel Hawthorne's *The Scarlet Letter* (1850) being an enduring example.

But even the most totalitarian Puritan *mores* could have their lighter side at sermon time, as Obadiah Turner noted in his journal for 3 June 1646:

> Allen Bridges hath bin chose to wake the sleepers in meeting. And being much proude of his place, must needs have a fox taile fixed to the ende of a long staff wherewith he may brush the faces of them that will have napps in time of discourse, likewise a sharpe thorne whereby he may pricke such as be most sound.
>
> On the last Lord his day, as hee strutted about the meeting-house, he did spy Mr Tomlins sleeping with much comfort, hys head kept steadie by being in the corner, and his hand grasping the rail. And soe spying, Allen did quickly thrust his staff behind Dame Ballard and give him a grievous prick upon the hand. Whereupon Mr Tomlins did spring upp much above the floore, and with terrible force strike hys hand against the wall; and also, to the great wonder of all, prophanlie exclaim in a loud voice, 'Curse the woodchuck', he dreaming so it seemed that a wood-chuck had seized and bit his hand. But on coming to know where he was, and the greate scandall he had committed, he seemed much abashed, but did not speak. And I think he will not soon again goe to sleepe in meeting.

As for the eighteenth century, it will, as far as religion goes, call to mind the Enlightenment, Deism, Voltaire and the Encyclopaedists, Rousseau and Hume, Wilkes and Tom Paine, atheism and revolution. And on the part of Christianity it is easy to remember the formalism of established worship, the money-grubbing of pluralist clergy enjoying the fruits of many benefices or of the ordinaries of the Fleet Prison joining all comers in matrimony for a fee. Intellectually, nominally Christian writers seemed to have sold the pass to rationalism. Alexander Pope (a Catholic at that) hardly goes beyond natural religion in his *Essay on Man*; the virtues of human speculation supply for the supernatural ends of revelation.

But there was another current flowing strongly during the eighteenth century which appealed to the emotions as much as to the intellect. In Italy Alphonsus Liguori provided the devotion and practical morality that his contemporaries hungered for. The cultural offensive that St Philip Neri launched through his Oratories, where music brought in people of taste (who might stay for a sermon or for acts of devotion), continued into the eighteenth century. In Protestant countries too there were other things to do in church than listen to sermons, as Bach's cantatas and sacred oratorios showed. Bach's tremendous achievement was known in his own lifetime only locally. Another Germanic influence brought music and devotion together for English-speaking audiences with Handel's sacred works; his *Messiah* (1742) won lasting popularity with English-speaking listeners, for whom the libretto seemed quite naturally to be expressed in their own language, like the Bible itself.

For private devotion Jeremy Taylor's *Holy Living* and *Holy Dying* continued to be popular in the century after their publication, and they remained a popular gift-book until after the close of the nineteenth century. Certainly Taylor's works changed lives. But it was another good book, William Law's *Serious Call to a Devout and Holy Life* (1729) that really shook the English-speaking world. It still stirred Newman's conscience nearly a century later, and in the meantime it persuaded other clever men that they should do something about the religion that everyone professed except a few outré atheists.

Law's book came out at just the time when John Wesley and his brother Charles were looking out for a more 'serious' way of being members of the Church of England. John Wesley went to see Law, who practised the devotion he preached, in 1732, and it was under Law's influence that the Wesleys made their brave but humanly disastrous missionary expedition to Georgia from 1735 to 1738. Wesley was later to have differences with Law, notably over mysticism – the practice and consequences of mental prayer – but always quoted Law in a friendly manner in his sermons. And if Wesley distrusted mystics, he did, in his widely hospitable reading, take to his heart *The Imitation of Christ*, the fifteenth-century work of devotion that secured a curiously enduring place in English hearts, in miniature editions accompanying many a soldier, with the Book of Common Prayer, in the terrible trenches of the First World War.

It is not quite the case that without Law there would have been no Methodism, but the success of Law showed that there was parched land in Britain and beyond that would soak up a thorough appeal to religious feelings. Wesley was the most astonishing evidence of this thirst. This is no place to tell his story, but he was an extraordinary man, who first began to feel old at the age of 85, having travelled on foot or horseback 225,000 miles and preached 40,000 sermons. Indeed he gave, as one of the reasons for his longevity, regular preaching, together with his ability to call up sleep whenever he wished. He hardly ever missed a night's sleep, but rose at four and preached at five. He read in the saddle, finding that in 100,000 miles only two horses ever gave him trouble when left thus on a loose rein. Ascetic in his life from the time he read Jeremy Taylor as a young man, Wesley declared towards the end of his life that he had experienced 'so little pain in my life and so little sorrow and anxious care'. With preaching as his chief means to convert and strengthen his followers, Wesley left at his death a body of worshippers in his own country numbering 70,000.

Methodism would never have been what it was without George Whitefield (1714–1770). It was he who started the practice of field preaching. He was regarded as a more convincing preacher than Wesley. The worldly Lord Chesterfield was moved on hearing him; even David Hume was impressed. Hearers mentioned his histrionic skill, his winning and audible voice. His sermons do not seem so remarkable in print. Whitefield crossed and recrossed the Atlantic and died at 56, but not before he had given an impetus to Christian revival in America. Although Wesley seemed generally untroubled by doctrinal differences, the fact was that Whitefield was a Calvinist and John Wesley was not. From 1741, their followers went different ways.

Of all Calvinist preachers, Jonathan Edwards is the most notorious, for the strength of his insistence on God's 'arbitrary will, restrained by no obligation' bringing so many to hell. Edwards spoke with great power on hell, asking his congregation to realize that 'God that holds you over the pit of hell, much as one holds a spider, or some loathsome insect over the fire, abhors you, and is dreadfully provoked'. It was not the way Wesley spoke.

It sometimes seems that Samuel Johnson belongs to an earlier world to John Wesley, whose movement so much changed the industrialized cities of Victorian Britain; but they were contemporaries, Johnson being six years younger. Johnson's importance lay partly in being a big figure in literature: he stood against the presumption of the enlightenment that clever people had outgrown God. Johnson was a man of encyclopaedic learning who opposed the rationalist Encyclopaedists. Moreover he was a layman. Just as he wrote articles on law for legal friends, he wrote sermons for clerical friends, and beat both professions at their own business. Yet it is not really as a spiritual writer that Johnson made his mark, but as a good man. He strove to overcome his defects (succeeding against drunkenness, if only by abstinence, not by moderation). We know that he was good – to the black boy Frank Barber, to the household of lame dogs that he sheltered, a blind woman, a bad-tempered old lady, a doctor to the ragged poor – but we know it not from Johnson's pen, but from Boswell's.

When Boswell asked Johnson which were the best English preachers for their style, he admitted these as pretty good: Atterbury, Tillotson, South, Seed, Jortin, Sherlock, Smallridge, Clarke, and possibly Ogden. (When Boswell took a copy of Ogden's sermons on prayer with him on their tour to the Hebrides, Johnson showed no eagerness to read it.) Now, no one to speak of reads these sermons today, nor have I chosen any to appear here.

The great fault of Johnson's contemporaries was generalization. They saw it as a virtue to discuss the generic, not the specific. Boswell picks out, as a *lively* account of the faculty of 'Wit', a passage from a sermon by Barrow 'Against Foolish talking and Jesting'. 'It raiseth admiration', says Barrow of wit, 'as signifying a nimble sagacity of apprehension, a special felicity of invention, a vivacity of spirit, and reach of wit more than vulgar; it seeming to argue a new quickness of parts, that one fetch in remote conceits applicable; a notable skill that he can dextrously accommodate them to the purpose before him; together with a lively briskness of humour, not apt to damp those sportful flashes of imagination.' There is a lot more of this.

Barrow was famous for his long sermons in an age of long sermons. He broke off one, on the duty of bounty to the poor, after three and a half hours, and on another occasion, in Westminster Abbey, the impatient vergers persuaded the organist to play loud and 'blow him down'. Barrow died in 1677, before the Augustan age was born, but his style belongs more to the next generation than to his father's. I am not saying that Barrow's style is thoroughly bad, but the modern reader tends to associate it with boredom because others have managed it much less well. Instead of getting what oft was thought but ne'er so well expressed, the reader is left with dull thoughts dressed in secondhand finery.

It is this dunce's dressing-up box that Sydney Smith satirized in the *Edinburgh Review*. The sermons of the later nineteenth and the twentieth century might be bad, but not in that way; in any case their language, being closer to our own usage, is clear to our gaze and shows up its flaws more clearly. Newman is reticent, nuanced, but he strives for the real, not the theory. Spurgeon spouts inexhaustibly, but he catches the ear of thousands of ordinary city dwellers. In our own day, H. A. Williams has said things in the pulpit that have struck some listeners as a denial of God's unchangeable law; but he is honest, he preaches what he has experienced.

★   ★   ★

This is not meant to be the sort of book that shops shelve under the label 'Inspirational'. Not everything in it is even true. There is stirring inspiration here for all that. And if you want to rummage further in the jumble of history there are mounds of sermons in good condition to sort through. The Fast Sermons delivered before the House of Commons between 1640 and 1660, for example, occupy 33 volumes, and a modern publisher has troubled to reproduce them.

Anyone interested in understanding the culture of past ages will find that sermons convey a sense of period otherwise only to be found in letters and diaries. This is how people thought.

SERMON ONE

Peter the Apostle

The Acts of the Apostles tells how the chosen followers of Jesus were gathered together in Jerusalem after his resurrection and his ascent into heaven. The house was filled with a sound like a rushing wind and they saw divided tongues of fire upon them. The apostles began to speak foreign languages, which were understood by people in the crowd from different countries. But some laughed at them, saying that they were full of new wine. Peter stood up with the other apostles and addressed the crowd.

Ye men of Judaea, and all ye that dwell at Jerusalem, be this known unto you, and hearken to my words. For these are not drunken as ye suppose, seeing it is but the third hour of the day. But this is that which was spoken by the prophet Joel: 'And it shall come to pass in the last days, saith God. I will pour out of my Spirit upon all flesh: and your sons and your daughters shall prophesy, and your young men shall see visions, and your old men shall dream dreams. And on my servants and on my hand-maidens I will pour out in those days of my Spirit; and they shall prophesy. And I will shew wonders in heaven above, and signs in the earth beneath; blood, and fire, and vapour of smoke; the sun shall be turned into darkness and the moon into blood before that great and notable day of the Lord come. And it shall come to pass, that whosoever shall call upon the name of the Lord shall be saved.'

Ye men of Israel, hear these words; Jesus of Nazareth, a man approved of God among you by miracles and wonders and signs, which God did by him in the midst of you, as ye yourselves also know: him being delivered by the determinate counsel and fore-knowledge of God, ye have taken, and by wicked hands have crucified and slain. Whom God hath raised up, having loosed the pains of death: because it was not possible that he should be holden of it. For David speaketh concerning him, 'I foresaw the Lord always before my face, for he is on my right hand, that I should not be moved. Therefore did my heart rejoice, and my tongue was glad: moreover also my flesh shall rest in hope: because thou wilt not leave my soul in hell, neither wilt thou suffer thine Holy One to see corruption. Thou hast made known to me the ways of life; thou shalt make me full of joy with thy countenance.'

Men and brethren, let me freely speak unto you of the patriarch David, that he is both dead and buried, and his sepulchre is with us unto this day. Therefore being a prophet and knowing that God had sworn with an oath to him, that of the fruit of his loins, according to the flesh, he would raise up Christ to sit on his throne; he seeing this before spake of the resurrection of Christ, that his soul was not left in hell, neither his flesh did see corruption.

This Jesus hath God raised up, whereof we all are witnesses. Therefore being by the right hand of God exalted, and having received of the Father the promise of the Holy Ghost, he hath shed forth this, which ye now see and hear.

For David is not ascended into the heavens: but he saith himself, 'The Lord said unto my Lord, Sit thou on my right hand, until I make thy foes thy footstool.' Therefore let all the house of Israel know assuredly that God hath made that same Jesus, whom ye have crucified, both Lord and Christ.

Acts 2:14–36 (AV)

The end in view

I write to you in the midst of life, enamoured of death. My Love has been crucified, and there is not within me any fire of earthly desire, but only water that lives and speaks in me, and says from within me: 'Come here to the Father.' I have no pleasure in the food of corruption nor in the pleasures of this material life. I desire God's bread, which is the flesh of Christ, who is of the seed of David, and for drink I desire his blood, which is love incorruptible.

St Ignatius of Antioch:
The Letter to the Romans, written on his way to martyrdom, in about AD 110

3

SERMON TWO

John Chrysostom

This sermon is remarkable for the dramatic circumstances in which it was delivered. John (347–407) was later given the name Chrysostom 'Golden-Mouthed' because of his wonderful preaching. His sermons were often interrupted by applause. He is revered as a saint, father and doctor of the Church. But his own faithfulness to Christian teaching and his fearless denunciation of the bad behaviour of the powerful got him into trouble, and he was to die under arrest in exile.

In 398 John was, against his own preference, made Bishop of Constantinople, the great eastern capital of the Roman Empire. His appointment was secured by Eutropius, a eunuch who had plotted his way from being an outcast slave to becoming the greatest power in the Empire, with more practical authority than the Emperor, Arcadius.

But Eutropius declared himself Consul to the horror and disgust of the Roman establishment. His fall came quickly when an army commander attempted a coup and marched on Constantinople. The commander of the city soldiery (like the invader a Goth, this being the era of barbarian incursions) was said to have declared that the capital could be saved only if Eutropius went.

The poor fellow, in well-founded fear of death, fled to the cathedral for sanctuary. By an irony he had earlier insisted on abolishing the right of the Church to grant it. But John now sent a formal delegation to the Emperor to assert this right.

The whole city, the biggest in the world, was abuzz with talk of Eutropius's fall and sanctuary. The next day, a Sunday, the cathedral was crowded by people eager to hear what John would say. They were not disappointed. As the Bishop took his place to preach, a curtain was thrown back to reveal the pitiful figure of Eutropius clutching at the pillars of the altar. Then John began to speak.

As an afterword: Eutropius tried to flee a few days later (although John guaranteed him sanctuary indefinitely), was caught on his way to Cyprus, tried for crimes against the state, and beheaded.

'Vanity of vanities, all is vanity' – this saying is always in season but more especially at the present time. Where are the brilliant surroundings of your consulship now? Where are the bright lights? Where is the dancing and the noise of dancers' feet, the banquets and the festivals? Where are the garlands of the theatre? Where is the applause which greeted you in the city, where the acclamation in the hippodrome and the flattery from spectators?

They are gone – all gone. A wind has blown upon the tree, bringing down all its leaves and showing it to us quite bare. So great has been the violence of the blast that it has strained every fibre of the tree and threatens to tear it up by the roots.

Where now are those who pretended to be your friends? Where are your drinking parties, and your suppers? Where is the swarm of parasites, and the wine that was poured out all day long, and all the dishes contrived by your cooks? Where are all the people who courted your influence, doing everything they could to win your favour?

They were all just visions of the night, and dreams which have vanished with the dawn. They were spring flowers, and when the spring was over they all withered. They were a shadow which has passed away. They were a smoke which has dispersed, bubbles which have burst, cobwebs which have been torn in pieces.

That is why we can always sing this spiritual chant 'Vanity of vanities, all is vanity.' This saying should always be written on our wills, on our clothes, in the market place, and in the house, in the streets, on the door and the gate – above all on the conscience of everyone. It must be a constant theme for meditation.

Deceit, masks and pretence seem to many people to be the real thing. So everyone every day, at breakfast and at supper, whenever he meets his neighbour should say to him and expect to hear in return: 'Vanity of vanities, all is vanity.'

Didn't I keep telling you, Eutropius, that wealth would run off? But you would not pay attention. Didn't I tell you that wealth was an ungrateful servant? But you would not be persuaded. Now you can see from experience that it has run away from you, that it is an ungrateful servant. Not only that but a murderous one, bringing you now to tremble here in fear.

When you kept criticising me for speaking the truth, did I not reply: 'I love you better than the people who flatter you. I may reprove you, but I care more for you than the people who pay court to you.' I said that a wound from a friend was more trustworthy than the kisses of enemies. If you had accepted a wound from me, their kisses would not have destroyed you. The wounds I offered were intended to bring you health; the kisses of those people have produced an incurable disease.

Where now are the men who waited on you? Where are the men who cleared the way for you in the crowded street? Where are the people who praised you in everyone's hearing all the time? They have gone, they have dropped your friendship. They are saving their own skins by landing you in it.

I have not behaved like that. In your misfortune I am not leaving you alone. Now you have fallen I am still protecting you and looking after you. The Church that you treated as an enemy has accepted you into her shelter. The theatres you once frequented – and about which you were often indignant with me – have betrayed you.

All along, I kept asking: 'Why do you do these things? You are provoking the Church and ruining yourself.' You would have none of my warnings. And now the hippodromes have exhausted your wealth and encouraged people to take up arms against you. But the Church which suffered your untimely anger is energetically trying to get you out of the trap into which you have fallen.

I'm not saying all this just to kick a man when he's down, but to keep whoever is still standing from falling. I am not rubbing the salt into the wound, but trying to preserve in sound health anyone who has not yet been wounded. I am not trying to sink a boat tossed by the waves, but to show whoever is sailing with a wind in the right direction how to remain on an even keel.

How can I do this? By pointing out the ups and downs of human affairs. Even Eutropius, if he had seen the dangers, would not have had such a fall. But neither his own conscience nor the advice of other people brought any improvement in him. So at least you who still count on your wealth can profit by seeing how disaster came his way. Nothing is less reliable than human plans.

Whatever name you give them, to express their feebleness, falls short of the reality. Smoke, or grass, or a dream, or spring flowers, or anything else. They are so perishable that they are less than nothing. Worse than being nothing they possess a very dangerous element. What we see before us shows this.

Who was higher than this man? Wasn't he richer than anyone else? Hadn't he climbed to the very summit of eminence? Wasn't everyone afraid of him? Look at him now, sadder than a prisoner, more pitiful than a slave, poorer than a starving beggar. Every day he has before him a vision of sharp swords and a criminal's grave, with the public executioner leading him out to his death. He hardly remembers if he once enjoyed pleasure. He scarcely feels the sunshine, but experiences nothing but the deepest gloom.

However much I try I shall not be able to express the suffering he must naturally be undergoing, as at each minute he expects death. But who needs my words, when you can see him here, the very image of misery?

Yesterday when they came for him from the royal court, meaning to drag him away, and he ran for refuge to the holy altar, his face was the same as it is now: pale as a corpse, his teeth chattering, his whole body shivering, his voice faltering and stammering. He was petrified.

I am not saying this to reproach him or mock his misfortune, but to soften your minds towards him, to make you feel compassion for him, to persuade you to be contented with the punishment which has already been inflicted. There are plenty of unkind people here who are inclined to blame me for having granted him sanctuary. I show you how much he has suffered to soften your hardheartedness.

Why, my dear brothers, are you indignant with me? You say it is because someone who always made war upon the Church has now taken refuge within it. Yet surely we ought to glorify God for permitting him to be in such straits as to experience both the strength and the loving kindness of the Church. Her strength, because he has suffered this great fall through of the attacks which he made upon her. Her loving kindness, because although he once attacked her she now shields him and shelters him under her wing. She keeps him safe without resenting any of the injuries he did her.

This loving kindness is more glorious than any trophy. It is a brilliant victory. It puts both Gentiles and Jews to shame. It shows the Church's brightest face: having been brought her enemy as a captive, she spares him. When everyone else despises him in his desolation, she alone like an affectionate mother hides him under her cloak. She opposes the king's anger, the people's rage and hatred.

But here is an ornament for the altar. A strange kind of ornament, you say – the accused sinner, the extortioner, the robber being permitted to lay hold of the altar. Don't talk like that! The prostitute took hold of the feet of Jesus, a woman who was stained with the most unclean sins. But what she did was no shame to Jesus, but rather showed him to be the more admirable. The impure woman did no harm to the man who was pure. Instead the unclean prostitute was made clean by the touch of the man who was the pure and spotless one.

Do not be so grudging, then. We are the servants of the crucified one who said: 'Forgive them for they know not what they do.'. . .

Let us rescue the captive, the fugitive, the suppliant from danger, that we ourselves may obtain the future blessings by the favour and mercy of our Lord Jesus Christ, to whom be glory and power, now and for ever, world without end. Amen.

Prayer for the Virgin's intercession, fourth century

Sub tuum praesidium confugimus, sancta Dei genitrix. Nostras deprecationes ne despicias in necessitatibus nostris, sed a periculis cunctis libera nos semper, Virgo gloriosa et benedicta.

We fly to your protection, holy Mother of God. Do not turn away as we make our entreaties in our great need, but always deliver us from all dangers, O glorious and Blessed Virgin.

Extract from an ancient homily for Holy Saturday: Christ's descent into the underworld

Something strange is happening. There is a great silence on earth today, a great silence and stillness. The whole earth keeps silence because the King is asleep.

The earth trembled and is still because God has fallen asleep in the flesh and he has raised up all who have slept ever since the world began. God has died in the flesh and hell trembles with fear. He has gone to search for our first parent, as for a lost sheep. Greatly desiring to visit those who live in darkness and in the shadow of death, he has gone to free from sorrow the captives Adam and Eve, he who is both God and the son of Eve.

The Lord approached them bearing the cross, the weapon that had won him the victory. At the sight of him Adam, the first man he had created, struck his breast in terror and cried out to everyone: 'My Lord be with you all.'

Christ answered him: 'And with your spirit.'

He took him by the hand and raised him up, saying: 'Sleeper, awake, and rise from the dead, and Christ will give you light. I am your God, who for your sake have become your son. Out of love for you and for your descendants I now by my own authority command all who are held in bondage to come forth, all who are in darkness to be enlightened, all who are sleeping to arise. I order you, O sleeper, to awake.

'I did not create you to be held a prisoner in hell. Rise from the dead, for I am the life of the dead. Rise up, work of my hands, you who were created in my image.

'Rise, let us leave this place, for you are in me and I am in you; together we form only one person and we cannot be separated.

'For your sake I, your God, became your son; I, the Lord, took the form of a slave; I, whose home is above the heavens, descended to the earth and beneath the earth. For your sake, for the sake of man, I became like a man without help, free among the dead. For the sake of you, who left a garden, I was betrayed to the Jews in a garden, and I was crucified in a garden.

'See on my face the spittle I received in order to restore to you the life I once breathed into you. See there the marks of the blows I received in order to refashion your damaged nature in my image. On my back see the marks of the scourging I endured to remove the burden of sin that weighs upon your back. See my hands, nailed fast to a tree, for you who once wickedly stretched out your hand to a tree.

'I slept on the cross and a sword pierced my side for you who slept in paradise and brought forth Eve from your side. My side has healed the pain in yours. My sleep will rouse you from your sleep in hell. The sword that pierced me has sheathed the sword that was turned against you.

'Rise, let us leave this place. The enemy led you out of the earthly paradise. I will not restore you to that paradise, but I will enthrone you in heaven.

'I forbade you the tree that was only a symbol of life, but see, I who am life itself am now one with you. I appointed cherubim to guard you as slaves are guarded, but now I make them worship you. The throne formed by cherubim awaits you, its bearers swift and eager.

'The bridal chamber is adorned, the banquet is ready, the eternal dwelling places are prepared, the treasure houses of all good things lie open.

'The kingdom of heaven has been prepared for you from all eternity.'

Christ is risen! He is risen indeed! Alleluia!

God's protection

I arise today:
in the might of Christ's birth and his baptism;
in the might of his crucifixion and burial
in the might of his resurrection and ascension
in the might of his descent to the judgement of doom.

Attributed to St Patrick (c. 389–461)

SERMON THREE

St Augustine

Augustine (354–430) lived in the part of North Africa called Numidia (now Tunisia and Algeria) when it was a thoroughly Roman province. He was an accomplished professional rhetorician, lived for fourteen years with a mistress in Carthage, and was converted, aged 34, to Christianity in Milan after coming under the influence of Ambrose, the bishop there.

Back in Africa he became Bishop of Hippo, a coastal city, in 396, and stayed there for the rest of his life. We still have 113 books that he wrote, including the autobiographical Confessions, *the influential* City of God *and volumes of brilliant theology. Augustine has been seen as the ideal bishop tending his flock. This is reflected in the hundreds of his surviving sermons. In many we hear his very voice, for they were taken down by trained shorthand writers.*

This extract, the first half of a sermon on John 9, the account of Jesus's giving of sight to the man born blind, exhibits some of the paradoxes and twists and turns that entertained an audience accustomed to listening to public speakers.

We have heard a reading of the Holy Gospel with which we are familiar. But it is a good thing to be reminded, good to refresh the memory from dull forgetfulness. Indeed this old familiar reading has given us as much pleasure as if it were new to us.

Christ gave sight to a man who was blind from his birth. Why are we surprised? Christ is the Saviour, and by an act of mercy he made up for something that he had not given this man when he was a child in the womb. When he gave that man no eyes to see, it was certainly not a mere mistake: he was looking forward to a future miracle.

Perhaps you are saying: 'Where do you get this information from?' I heard it from Christ himself. He said it just now. All of us here together heard it. When his disciples asked him: 'Master, who did sin, this man or his parents, that he was born blind?', you heard the answer he made, as I did. 'Neither hath this man sinned, nor his parents, but that the works of God should be made manifest in him.'

That, then, was why Christ delayed giving him the sight of his eyes. He did not give him what he could give; he did not give him what he knew he would give when need was. Yet do not suppose, brothers, that this man's parents had no sin, or that he himself had not, when he was born, contracted original sin (for the remission of which infants are baptised). But his blindness was not the consequence of his parents' sin, nor of his own sin. It was 'that the works of God should be made manifest in him'. When we were born we were all affected by original sin, and yet we were not born blind.

Think about it carefully, though, and you will realize that we were born blind. Who was not born blind – blind, that is, in heart? Yet the Lord Jesus, since he created both eyes and heart, cured both.

★   ★   ★

With the eyes of faith you have seen this blind man. You have also heard him erring. I will tell you how he erred. First, he thought Christ a prophet, and did not know that he was the Son of God. And then we have heard him give an answer that is entirely false, when he said: 'We know that God heareth not sinners.' If God does not hear sinners, what hope have we? If God does not hear sinners, why do we pray and make public the record of our sin by beating the breast? And where would it leave that Publican, who went up with the Pharisee into the Temple? While the Pharisee was boasting and parading his own merits, he stood far off, with his eyes fastened on the ground, beating his breast and confessing his sins. This man, who confessed his sins, went down from the Temple justified rather than the Pharisee. So God certainly does hear sinners.

But the blind man who gave that answer had not yet washed the face of his heart in Siloam. The mystical sign had been performed on his eyes; but in his heart it had not yet worked the blessing of grace. When did this blind man wash the face of his heart? When the Lord admitted him to himself after he had been cast out by the Jews. For the Lord found him, and said to him as we have heard: 'Dost thou believe on the Son of God?'

He replied: 'Who is he, Lord, that I may believe on him?' With his eyes, it is true, he could see already. But could he see him yet in his heart? No, not yet. Wait, he will see him presently.

Jesus answered: 'I that speak with thee am he.' Did he doubt? No, with that, he washed his face. For he was speaking with the very Siloam 'which is by interpretation, "Sent".' Who is the one Sent, but Christ? He often bore witness to that by saying: 'I do the will of my Father that sent me.' He himself, then was Siloam. The man came to him blind in heart. He heard and believed, adored, washed his face, and saw.

Night prayer

Qui placido in puppi carpebat pectore somnum,
Exurgens ventis imperat et pelago:
Fessa labore gravi quamvis hic membra quiescent,
Ad se concedat cor vigilare meum.
Agne dei, mundi qui crimina cuncta tulisti,
Conserva requiem mitis ab hoste meam.

He lay with quiet heart in the stern asleep:
Waking, commanded both the winds and sea.
Christ, though this weary body slumber deep,
Grant that my heart may keep its watch with thee.
O Lamb of God that carried all our sin,
Guard thou my sleep against the enemy.

Alcuin (translated by Helen Waddell)

Alcuin (735–804) left St Peter's school at York in 785 to take over Charlemagne's palace school at Aachen. He retired to St Martin's at Tours in 796 and prepared an accurate edition of the Vulgate Bible (a copy of which is in the British Museum) as a gift for Charlemagne on his coronation by the Pope on Christmas Day 800. Alcuin left a line of scholars who endured through the centuries.

SERMON FOUR

❧

Aelfric

Aelfric lived from about 955 to 1020. His name is pronounced Alfritch. He became a monk at Cerne Abbas, Dorset, and later the first Abbot of Eynsham in Oxfordshire. English piety and preaching had thriven continuously from the time of the missionary journey of Augustine of Canterbury at the end of the sixth century, interrupted by such periodic violence as the Viking attacks. One of these led to the death of King Edmund of the East Angles in 870. He was counted a martyr and his relics were transferred to the town subsequently known as Bury St Edmunds, in Suffolk, where the ruins of his shrine remain. For his saint's day on 20 November, Aelfric wrote one of his series of sermons that exemplify the poetic quality of Anglo-Saxon prose designed to be delivered orally. He spoke in English, but English has changed a good deal in the 1,000 years since then. The lines of this poetic prose are pinned together by alliteration, usually with a rhythmic pause in the middle of each line. So in describing the tomb robbers miraculously frozen in position, Aelfric says:

Ne hi thanon astyrian, ac stodon swa oth mergen.
Men tha thaes wundrodon hu tha weargas hangodon

*Nor could they stir from there, but stood like that till morning.
People wondered then why those wretches were hanging there.*

St Edmund, King and Martyr
(20 November)

A learned monk came from the South, over the sea, from Saint Benedict's Stow, in the days of King Aethelred, to Archbishop Dunstan, three years before he died; and the monk was called Abbo. They were in conversation when Dunstan told him about St Edmund, even as Edmund's sword-bearer had told the events to King Aethelstan when Dunstan was a young man and the sword-bearer a very old man. Then the monk put all this story in a book, and when the book had come to us, we turned it after a few years into English. This monk Abbo within two years went home to his monastery, and was almost immediately appointed abbot there.

> Edmund the blessed, king of the East Angles,
> was wise and honourable, and through his excellent
>   conduct
> always gave glory to Almighty God.
> He was humble and devout, and continued so steadfast
> that he would not yield to shameful sins,
> nor in any way depart from his practices,
> but was always mindful of true doctrine . . .
> One day a messenger came from Hingwar the seaman
> who said: Hingwar has landed here now with an army,
> to take up his winter-quarters here with his men.
> He commands you to divide your secret treasure
> and your ancestors' wealth with him.
> And you shall be his under-king, if you wish to live,
> for you do not have the power to withstand him . . .
> Edmund turned to the messenger and said:
> Go quickly, and say to your cruel lord:
> Edmund the king will never bow in life to Hingwar
> the heathen leader, unless he will first bow,
> in this land, to Jesus Christ with faith.
> Then the messenger hurried away,
> and met on the way the bloodthirsty Hingwar
> with all his army marching on Edmund,
> and told that wicked man the reply.
> Hingwar then arrogantly commanded his troops
> to go all together and take the king alone,
> since he had despised his command, and instantly bind him.
> Edmund the king, when Hingwar came,
> stood within his hall, and mindful of the Saviour,
> threw away his weapons, desiring to imitate
> Christ's example, who forbade Peter
> to fight with weapons against the Jews.

Then those wicked men bound Edmund,
and shamefully insulted him, and beat him with clubs,
and afterward they led the faithful king
to a tree rooted in the earth, and tied him to it
with hard bonds. And they scourged him
for a long time, and he called out,
on Jesus Christ between the blows,
with true faith. And then the heathen
because of his faith were full of anger,
because he called upon Christ to help him.
They shot at him with arrows as if for amusement,
until he was all beset with them,
as with a porcupine's bristles, as Sebastian was.
When Hingwar, the wicked seaman,
saw that the noble king would not deny Christ,
but with steadfast faith called upon him,
he commanded his men to behead him, and so the
    heathen did.
While he was still calling upon Christ,
the heathen came to the saint, to kill him,
and with one blow struck off his head.
And his soul departed joyfully to Christ.
There was a certain man at hand, hidden
by God from the heathen, who heard all this,
and told it afterward even as I tell it.
So then the seamen withdrew to their ship,
having hidden the head of the holy Edmund
in the thick brambles, that it might not be buried.
Then after a while, when they were gone away,
the country people who were still left came
to where their lord's body lay headless.
And they were heartbroken at his murder,
and at finding the body without the head.
Then the man who had seen everything said
that the seamen had taken the head with them,
and it seemed to him likely that they

had hidden the head somewhere about.
Then they all went looking for it in the wood,
searching among the thorns and brambles
to see if they could find the head anywhere.
A great wonder happened then, for a wolf was sent
by God's direction, to guard the head
against the other animals by day and night.
Those that sought it went about crying out,
as is the way with people who go through woods:
'Where are you now, comrade?' And the head
    answered them,
'Here, here, here.' And so it cried out
answering them whenever they shouted,
until they came upon it by means of those cries.
There lay the grey wolf who guarded the head,
with his two feet he embraced the head.
Though he was fiercely hungry, God's power
    prevented him
from tasting the head. He protected it from other animals.
The people were astonished at the wolf's guardianship,
and carried the holy head home with them,
thanking the Almighty for all his wonders.
The wolf followed them with the head
until they came to the town, as if he were tame,
and then turned back again to the wood.
Then the country people laid the head
by the holy body, and buried him
as well as they might in such haste.
Then again, after many years,
when the seamen's harrying had ceased, and peace
    was restored
to the oppressed people, they came together,
and built a church worthy to the saint,
because miracles were frequently done at his burial-place,
at the house of prayer where he was buried.
Then they wanted to carry the holy body

with all honour, to lay it within the church.
Then they found a great wonder: that he was as whole
as if he were alive, with a body unbroken,
and the neck healed where it had been cut through,
though there was as it were a silken thread of red about
    his neck
as if to show men how he was slain.
The wounds which the bloodthirsty heathen
had made in his body by their repeated shots,
were healed by the God of heaven.
And so he lies uncorrupt until this present day,
awaiting the resurrection and eternal glory.
His body shows us, through lying undecayed,
that he lived without uncleanness here in the world,
and by a pure life passed to Christ.
A certain widow called Oswyn
lived near the saint's burial-place, in prayers
and fasting for many a year.
Every year she would cut the hair of the saint,
and cut his nails carefully and lovingly,
and keep them in a shrine as relics on the altar.
The people faithfully venerated the saint;
and Bishop Theodred greatly enriched the church
with gifts in gold and silver, in the saint's honour.
Then one day some unblessed thieves came,
eight of them in the night, to the venerable saint,
meaning to steal the treasures people had brought.
They tried to see how they could get in.
One struck at the hasp violently with a hammer;
one filed at it with a file;
one dug under the door with a spade;
one on a ladder tried to unlock the window.
But they worked in vain and got nowhere,
because the holy man miraculously froze them,
each as he stood, at work with his implement
so that none of them could accomplish that evil deed.

Nor could they stir from there, but stood like that
    till morning.
People wondered why those wretches were hanging there,
one on a ladder, one bent down to his digging,
and each frozen in the middle of his work.
They were all brought to the bishop,
and he commanded them to be hanged on high gallows.
But he did not bring to mind how merciful God
had spoken through his prophet these words:
Eos qui ducuntur ad mortem eruere ne cesses:
always deliver those who are led to death.
And the holy canons forbid clerics,
whether bishops or priests, to be concerned about thieves,
because it does not befit those chosen
for the service of God, to consent
to any man's death, if they are the Lord's servants.
Then Bishop Theodred, after he had consulted his books,
regretted that he had awarded such a cruel fate
to those unhappy thieves. He deplored it
to his life's end; and prayed that the people
might fast with him for three full days,
praying that the Almighty should have pity on him . . .
The English nation is not deprived of the Lord's saints,
since in this land lie such holy ones
as this saintly king, and the blessed Cuthbert,
and saint Etheldreda in Ely, and also her sister,
incorrupt in body, to confirm our faith.
There are many other saints among the English
who work many miracles, as is widely known,
to the glory of the Almighty in whom they believed.
Christ shows men where the true faith is,
for he works such miracles through his saints
throughout the earth. So to him be glory
with his heavenly Father, and with the Holy Spirit,
for ever and ever. Amen

Watch over me

Dunstanum memet clemens rogo Christe tuae
Tenarias me non sinas sorbisse porcellas.

I ask you, merciful Christ, to watch over me, Dunstan. May you
not permit the Taenarian storms to swallow me.

St Dunstan (924–988)

From the frontispiece of the so-called Class Book of St Dunstan, *written
in his own hand under a drawing of himself worshipping Christ. The first
line adapts words by Hrabanus Maurus, and the second line makes reference to the entrance to the underworld in the* Thebaid *by Statius. The
manuscript is in the Bodleian Library, Oxford.*

SERMON FIVE

St Bernard

Bernard (1090–1153) took a leading part in simplifying the monastic life, with the intention of attaining a closer union with God. He enthusiastically joined the strand of monastic life begun at Cîteaux, which gave its name to the Cistercian movement that gave medieval England and the rest of Europe much of its shape. Bernard was a friend of the monk who became Pope Eugenius III in 1145, and drew up for Eugenius a treatise on the ideals of the papacy. Though Bernard was continually sick, he stirred Europe into the second crusade, and dozens of new foundations were made from his own monastery of Clairvaux. Bernard appealed to the heart. His celebrated sermons on the Song of Solomon were a continuous commentary given daily to monks at prayer. Of course Bernard knew the literal meaning of the lover and the beloved, the bride and groom, but he applies it to God's life in the soul, of which he had deep knowledge, despite his bashfulness.

Return, my Beloved
(Song of Solomon 2:17)

She says, 'Return.' It is clear that the one she calls upon to return is not present; and yet that he had been present not long before, for she seems to call him back in the moment of his departure. To call someone back at such a moment shows the great love of the one and the great attraction of the other. Who follows charity with devoted and untiring affection that allows no rest in the pursuit of it?

I remember that I promised to apply this verse to the Word and to the soul; but I confess that I have great need of the help of the Word himself if this is to be done with anything even approaching a worthy treatment of the subject. Certainly it is a task that would suit someone with more experience and a fuller knowledge of the secrets of divine love than I. But I cannot refuse to attempt what my office requires of me, or turn down your requests.

I see the danger before me, but you oblige me, so I cannot avoid it. You oblige me (as the Psalmist says) to exercise myself in great matters, and in things too high for me . . .

'Return,' says the bride. He has gone; he is called back. Who will show me what this inconstancy means? Who can explain the going and the returning of the Word? Surely there can be no inconstancy in the Bridegroom? Where can he go, where can he return from, the one who fills all things? What movement in space can there be for him who is spirit? What movement of any kind whatsoever can be attributed to him who is God? He is absolutely immutable.

Let anyone who can understand these things who is capable of it. But let us in the exposition of this sacred and mystical discourse proceed carefully and with simplicity of purpose. We shall follow the example of Scripture itself, which declares the hidden wisdom in our human words certainly, but in a mystical way. In order to make God known to our powers of apprehension, it makes use of figurative language, and brings to human minds those precious truths, the unknown and invisible things of God, by means of similes drawn from sense data. We are offered, as it were, a draught of truth in cups of base matter.

Let us, then, follow the example of this discourse; let us say that the Word of God, who is God and the bridegroom of the soul, comes and goes to and from the soul as it pleases him. Only we must bear in mind that these events take place in the inward sense of the soul, not through any movements of the Word. For example, when the soul feels the influence of grace, it recognizes that the Word is present; and when it does not feel this influence, it complains of his absence, and asks him to return again, saying with the Psalmist: 'My heart said unto thee, thy face, Lord, will I seek.'

And how should the soul do anything else but seek him, since when that spouse (so dearly loved by her) is absent, she cannot – I do not say wish for, but even think of anyone else. There is nothing for her but to seek him earnestly when he is absent, to call him back when he departs. In this way, then, the Word is called back; that is to say, by the earnest longing of the soul, by the soul which has once had the happiness to taste how sweet is his goodness. Is not an earnest desire a voice? It is indeed, and a powerful one. For the Lord, says the Psalmist, has 'heard the desire of the humble'. When, then, the Word goes away, the one constant cry of the soul, its single desire, is a repeated 'Return' – until he comes.

Show me now a soul that the Bridegroom-Word visits frequently, to whom close knowledge of him has given boldness, in whom tasting has caused hunger, and I shall instantly assign to it the voice and the name of Bride. I shall apply to it the words that we are here considering. Such is, in fact, she who is here introduced as speaking.

For she gives sufficient proof, in calling back the Bridegroom, that she has merited his presence, although not the full abundance of his graces. For otherwise it would be a call, not a recall, that she would give. That it is here a recall is shown by the word 'Return'. Perhaps he withdrew himself for that very reason, that he might be called back with the greater eagerness, and clasped the more firmly. For when he sometimes makes it appear that he is to depart further away, it is not that he wants to do so, but so that he may hear: 'Lord, stay with us, for it is towards evening, and the day is far spent.' And, again, on another occasion, when he was walking on the sea and the Apostles were in a boat and toiling hard in rowing, he made as though he would have passed by them, though he did not indeed want to do so, but rather to prove their faith and draw out their prayer. For as the Evangelist puts it: 'They were troubled, and cried out, supposing that it had been a spirit.'

That holy simulation, or rather that attitude full of saving grace, which the Word, then in the body, sometimes made use of – the same Word (who is Spirit) does not cease to employ, though in a spiritual manner, with a soul that is devoted to him. When he seems to pass by, he wants to be detained, and when absent to be recalled. For he, who is the Word of God, is not irrevocable. He goes and returns according to his pleasure. He visits a soul at the breaking of the day, and suddenly puts the soul to the proof by withdrawing himself. If he comes into a soul, it is the effect of his free and spontaneous grace. If he retire from it, it is similarly according to his will. But both the one and the other depend upon his judgement, and of this he alone knows the ground and reason . . .

Come, Creator Spirit

Lava quod est sordidum,   *Da tuis fidelium,*
Riga quod est aridum,   *In te confidentibus,*
Sana quod est saucium.   *Sacrum septenarium.*
Flecte quod est rigidum,   *Da virtutis meritum*
Fove quod est frigidum,   *Da salutis exitum*
Rege quod est devium.   *Da perenne gaudium.*

Wash what is stained, water what is parched, heal what is wounded. Bend what is stiff, warm what is frozen, straighten what is crooked. Give your seven holy gifts to the faithful who put their trust in you. Give them reward for their virtue. Give them salvation at the end. Give them lasting happiness.

Conclusion to the Sequence for Whitsun
by Stephen Langton, Archbishop of Canterbury (1150–1228)

Sermon notes by Thomas Aquinas for the feast of St Bartholomew the Apostle

He hath barked my fig-tree, the branches thereof are made white. (Joel 1:7)

These words can be explained of St Bartholomew and his passion. Firstly, he who suffered is 'my fig-tree'. Secondly, the passion itself is expressed by 'he hath barked'. Thirdly, his reward by the words 'the branches thereof are made white'.

First Head

On the first head it is to be noted, that St Bartholomew can be likened to a fig-tree for three reasons, since it contains wood, leaves, and fruit.

I First reason

By the wood of the fig-tree is signified the holiness of his heart. The wood contains (1) the pith, (2) the fibre, and (3) the bark.

1. The pith has whiteness, which in the holy heart is the whiteness or candour of faith. 'The brightness of the everlasting light, the unspotted mirror of the power of God' (Wisdom, chapter 7, verse 26).
2. The woody fibre has fortitude or strength, which becomes the strength of hope in a holy soul. 'In quietness and confidence shall be your strength' (Isaiah, chapter 30, verse 15).
3. The bark preserves both the pith and the fibre; in a holy soul it is that preservation by love which leads onwards to the desire of heavenly things. 'Who shall separate us from the love of Christ?' (Epistle to the Romans, chapter 8, verse 35).

II Second reason

By the leaves of the fig-tree is signified the profitableness of speech. They have three qualities.

1. Milkiness of juice. This signifies purity of speech, since milk is white, and this purity comes from truth. 'The words of the pure are pleasant words' (Proverbs, chapter 15, verse 26).
2. Greenness in colour. This signifies the honesty from which flows the pleasure in speech, for green is a pleasing colour. 'Pleasant words, are as an honeycomb' (Proverbs, chapter 16, verse 24).
3. Roughness to the touch. This signifies that sharpness of speech which is often so useful and necessary. Bland words are often harmful and seductive; it is the rough speech which profits and

corrects. 'Let no corrupt communication proceed out of your mouth' (Epistle to the Ephesians, chapter 4, verse 29).

III Third reason
By the fruit of the fig-tree is signified holiness of action. Fruit has three qualities.

1. An internal redness. This signifies that charity in which all our actions ought to be performed. 'Let all your things be done with charity' (Epistle to the Romans, chaper 16, verse 14).
2. An external greenness, which is a middle colour, not in excess or defect. Green signifies humility, and this grace relieving our service of excess or defect. 'Which is your reasonable service' (Epistle to the Romans, chapter 12, verse 1).
3. A sweetness of taste, which signifies that joy in action which should accompany all our works. 'Not grudgingly or of necessity, for God loveth a cheerful giver' (Second Epistle to the Corinthians, chapter 9, verse 7).

Second Head
On the second head is to be noted the passion of St Bartholomew, who was 'barked' or flayed for three reasons.

I First reason
That he might be offered to God as a true lamb for a burnt offering. He shall flay the burnt offering and cut it into his pieces' (Leviticus, chapter 1, verse 6).

II Second reason
That he might be dried from every humour of sin, as the tree is barked to dry the wood. 'Do men gather figs of thistles?' (Gospel of St Matthew, chapter 7, verse 16).

III Third reason

He was flayed that he might be renewed like the serpent is when it has cast off its old skin. 'Be ye therefore wise as serpents' (Gospel of St Matthew, chapter 10, verse 16).

Third Head

On the third head is to be noted his reward: 'The branches thereof are made white.' They are four.

Firstly, the branches of the body, the bodily senses. These are whitened, for whosoever is holy shall receive delight.

Secondly, the branches of the mind are three: (1) the memory, (2) the intelligence, (3) the will.

1. The memory is whitened by the comprehension of eternity.
2. The intelligence, by the understanding of all truth.
3. The will, by the enjoyment of all that is desirable.

To be whitened both in body and soul is nothing else than to be glorified by the reception of white clothing. 'These are they which came out of great tribulation, and have washed their robes and made them white in the blood of the Lamb' (Revelation, chapter 7, verse 14).

Prayer of giving

O Divine Master, grant that I may not so much seek
to be consoled as to console,
to be understood as to understand,
to be loved as to love;
for it is in giving that we receive,
it is in pardoning that we are pardoned,
it is in dying that we are born to eternal life.

Francis of Assisi (1182–1226)

Private devotions

Our fader that art in heven sanctified be thy name. Thy kyngdom come to us. Thy wyl be done in erth as in heven. Our dayly breed gyve us to day, and forgyve us our dettes as we forgyve our dettors. And lede us not in to temptation, but delyver us from evyl. Amen

From *The Art or Crafte to Lyve Well*, printed by Wynkyn de Worde in 1505

As the Middle Ages went on, more lay people liked to use books of devotion, increasingly in their own language, not Latin. With the invention of printing in the fifteenth century such primers of prayer grew cheaper. Wynkyn de Worde was an apprentice of Caxton's.

SERMON SIX

The Homilies

The first volume of Homilies was published by state authority in July 1547, six months after the accession of Edward VI, 'for stay of such errors as were then by ignorant preachers sparkled among the people'. Unless they were licensed to preach, incumbents of parishes were obliged to read out parts of the Homilies each Sunday. There is no doubt that the Homilies incorporated doctrines of the reformers.

A second volume of Homilies was published in the fourth year of the reign of Elizabeth I, in 1562, at the same time as the Thirty-Nine Articles, the 35th of which directs that both volumes be read out in church 'diligently and distinctly'.

The Homilies' sermon for rogation week is cobbled together in three parts from sermons on several different texts; to these are added the exhortation below. It might now seem a strange choice to include in Elizabeth's Second Book of Homilies, but we must realize how important Rogation Day, with its procession from boundary marker to boundary marker, was to the predominantly agricultural England of the time. The anonymous homilist is careful to keep the congregation to their task, away from the communal celebration of patron saints that had distinguished rural life under Catholic monarchs, including Queen Mary, who had died not long before, in 1558.

The author uses certain agricultural terms unfamiliar now – doles, bierbalks, terries, livelodes, shack and ear – and which would certainly have puzzled congregations at the time in regions that had their own words for such things.

An Exhortation to be spoken to such parishes where they use their perambulations in Rogation Week for the oversight of the bounds and limits of their towns.

⋆   ⋆   ⋆

Although we be now assembled together, good Christian people, most principally to laud and thank Almighty God for his great benefits, by beholding the fields replenished with all manner fruits, to the maintenance of our corporal necessities, for our food and sustenance; and partly also to make our humble suits in prayers to his fatherly providence, to conserve the same fruits, in sending us seasonable weather, whereby we may gather in the said fruits to that end for which his merciful goodness hath provided them; yet have we occasion secondarily given us in our walks on these days to consider the old ancient bounds and limits belonging to our own township and to other our neighbours bordering about us, to the intent that we should be content with our own, and not contentiously strive for others, to the breach of charity, by any encroaching one upon another, or claiming one of the other further than that in ancient right and custom our forefathers have peaceably laid out unto us for our commodity and comfort . . .

★   ★   ★

'Thou shall not', commandeth Almighty God in his Law, 'remove thy neighbour's mark, which they of old time have set in thine inheritance.' 'Thou shall not', saith Salomon, 'remove the ancient bounds which thy fathers have laid.' And, lest we should esteem it to be but a light offence so to do, we shall understand that it is reckoned among the curses of God pronounced upon sinners. 'Accursed be he', saith Almighty God by Moses, 'who removeth his neighbour's doles and marks': and all people shall say, answering 'Amen' thereto, as ratifying that curse upon whom it doth light. They do much provoke the wrath of God upon themselves, which use to grind up the doles and marks which of ancient time were laid for division of meres and balks in the fields, to bring the owners to their right. They do wickedly which do turn up the ancient terries of the fields, that old men beforetime with great pains did tread out; whereby the lord's records (which be the tenant's evidences) be perverted and translated, sometime to the disheriting of the right owner, to the oppression of the poor fatherless or the poor widow. These covetous men know not what inconveniences they be authors of. Sometime by such craft and deceit be committed great discords and riots in the challenge of their lands, yea, sometime murders and bloodshed; whereof thou art guilty, whosoever thou be that givest the occasion thereof.

This covetous practising therefore with thy neighbour's lands and goods is hateful to Almighty God. 'Let no man subtilly compass or defraud his neighbour', biddeth St Paul, 'in any manner of cause. For God', saith he, 'is a revenger of all such.' God is the God of all equity and righteousness, and therefore forbiddeth all such deceit and subtilty in his Law by these words: 'Ye shall not do unjustly in judgment, in line, in weight, or measure: you shall have just balances, true weights, and true measures. False balance', saith Salomon, 'are an abomination unto the Lord.' Remember what St Paul saith, 'God is the revenger' of all wrong and injustice; as we see by daily experience, however it thriveth ungraciously which is gotten by falsehood and craft. We be taught by experience, how Almighty God never suffereth the third heir to enjoy his father's wrong possessions; yea, many a time they are taken from himself in his own lifetime. God is not bound to defend such possessions as be gotten by the devil and his counsel. God will defend all such men's goods and possessions which by him are obtained and possessed, and will defend them against the violent oppressor. So witnesseth Salomon: 'The Lord will destroy the house of the proud man; but he will stablish the borders of the widow.' 'No doubt of it,' saith David, 'better is a little truly gotten to the righteous man, than the innumerable riches of the wrongful man.' Let us flee therefore, good people, all wrong practices in getting, maintaining, and defending our possessions, lands, and livelodes, our bounds and liberties, remembering that such possessions be all under God's revengeance.

But what do I speak of house and land? Nay, it is said in Scriptures, that God in his ire doth root up whole kingdoms for wrongs and oppressions, and doth translate kingdoms from one nation to another for unrighteous dealing, for wrongs and riches gotten by deceit. This is the practice of the Holy One, saith Daniel, 'to the intent that living men may know, that the Most High hath power on the kingdoms of men, and giveth them to whomsoever he will'. Furthermore, what is the cause of penury and scarceness, of dearth and famine – any other thing but a token of God's ire, revenging our wrongs and injuries one done to another? 'Ye have sown much,' upbraideth God by his Prophet Aggei, 'and yet bring in little; ye eat, but ye be not satisfied; ye drink, but ye be not filled; ye clothe yourselves, but ye be not warm; and he that earneth his wages putteth it in a bottomless purse. Ye look for much increase, but lo, it came to little; and, when ye brought it home into your barns, I did blow it away, saith the Lord.' O consider therefore the ire of God against gleaners, gatherers, and incroachers upon other men's lands and possessions!

It is lamentable to see in some places, how greedy men use to plough and grate upon their neighbour's land that lieth next them; how covetous men nowadays plough up so nigh the common balks and walks, which good men beforetime made the greater and broader, partly for the commodious walk of his neighbour, partly for the better shack in harvest time to the more comfort of his poor neighbour's cattle. It is a shame to behold the insatiableness of some covetous persons in their doings; that where their ancestors left of their land a broad and sufficient bierbalk to carry the corpse to the Christian sepulture, how men pinch at such bierbalks, which by long use and custom ought to be inviolably kept for that purpose; and now they either quite tear them up, and turn the dead body to be borne further about in the high streets, or else, if they leave any such mere, it is too strait for two to walk on. These strange incroachments, good neighbours, should be looked upon, these should be considered, in these days of our perambulations; and afterward the parties monished and charitably reformed, who be the doers of such private gaining to the slander of the township and to the hinderance of the poor.

Your highways should be considered in your walks, to understand where to bestow your days' works according to the good statutes provided for the same. It is a good deed of mercy to amend the dangerous and noisome ways, whereby thy poor neighbour, sitting on his seely weak beast, foundereth not in the deep thereof, and so the market is the worse served for discouraging of poor victuallers to resort thither for the same cause.

If now therefore ye will have your prayers heard before Almighty God for the increase of your corn and cattle, and for the defence thereof from unseasonable mists and blasts, from hail and other such tempests, love equity and righteousness, ensue mercy and charity, which God most requireth at our hands. Which Almighty God respected chiefly in making his civil laws for his people the Israelites, in charging the owners not to gather up their corn too nigh at harvest season, nor the grapes and olives in gathering time, but to leave behind some ears of corn for the poor gleaners. By this he meant to induce them to pity the poor, to relieve the needy, to shew mercy and kindness. It cannot be lost which for his sake is distributed to the poor. 'For he which ministereth seed to the sower and bread to the hungry, which sendeth down the early and latter rain' upon your fields, so to fill up 'the barns with corn and the winepresses with wine and oil'; he, I say, who recompenseth all kind benefits 'in the resurrection of the just'; he will assuredly recompense all merciful deeds shewed to the needy, howsoever unable the poor is upon whom it is bestowed. 'O', saith Salomon, 'let not mercy and truth forsake thee. Bind them about they neck, saith he, and write them on the table of thy heart: so shalt thou find favour at God's hand. Thus honour thou the Lord with thy riches, and with the firstfruits of thine increase: so shall thy barns be filled with abundance, and thy presses shall burst with new wine.'

Nay, God hath promised to 'open the windows of heaven' upon the liberal righteous man, that he shall want nothing. He will repress the devouring caterpillar, which should devour your fruits. He will give you peace and quiet to gather in your provision, that ye may 'sit every man under his own vine' quietly, without fear of the foreign enemies to invade you. He will give you, not only food to feed on, but stomachs and good appetites to take comfort of your fruits, whereby in all things ye may have sufficiency. Finally, he will bless you with all manner abundance in this transitory life, and endue you with all manner benediction in the next world, in the kingdom of heaven, through the merits of our Lord and Saviour. To whom with the Father and the Holy Ghost be all honour everlastingly. Amen.

Patience works

Let nothing disturb you,
Let nothing dismay you,
All things pass.
God never changes.
Patience
Attains everything.
Whoever has God
Lacks nothing.
God alone suffices.

St Teresa of Avila (1515–1582)

SERMON SEVEN

Lancelot Andrewes

The memorial and tomb of Lancelot Andrewes (1555–1626) is to be seen in Southwark Cathedral, which in his day was a collegiate church near to the Thames-side palace in which he lived as Bishop of Winchester. An extraordinarily learned man, who mastered fifteen languages and had wide knowledge of the ancient Fathers of the Church, Andrewes helped write the Authorised Version of the Bible of 1611. He valued the sacraments, aimed at virtue and was a prayerful man; after his death his prayer book, Preces Privatae, in Hebrew, Greek and Latin, became a best-seller. As a preacher he loved word-play and liked to bring in Latin references. But he immediately says what the Latin words mean. The sense is immediately clear if the text is read aloud. He preached undaunted for twenty years before James I of England (VI of Scotland). The following half of the Christmas sermon for 1622 includes a sentence that Eliot uses in 'The Journey of the Magi': 'A cold coming . . .'.

A Sermon preached before the King's Majesty, at Whitehall, on Wednesday, the Twenty-Fifth of December, AD MDCXXII, being Christmas-Day.

> Behold there came wise men from the East to Jerusalem, saying, Where is the King of the Jews that is born? For we have seen his star in the East, and are come to worship Him (Matthew 2:1). (*Ecce magi ab Oriente venerunt Jerosolymam, dicentes: Ubi est qui natus est Rex Judaeorum? Vidimus enim stellam Eius in Oriente, et venimus adorare Eum.*)

This text may seem to come a little too soon, before the time; and should have stayed till the day it was spoken on, rather than on this day. But if you mark them well, there are in the verse four words that be proper and peculiar to this very day. 1. For first, *natus est* is most proper to this day of all days, the day of His Nativity. 2. Secondly, *vidimus stellam*; for on this day it was first seen, appeared first. 3. Thirdly, *venimus*, for this day they set forth, began their journey. 4. And last, *adorare Eum*, for 'when He brought His only-begotten Son into the world, He gave in charge, Let all the Angels of God worship Him.' And when the Angels to do it, no time more proper for us to do it as then. So these four appropriate it to this day, and none but this.

★   ★   ★

The main heads of their errand are (1) *Vidimus stellam*, the occasion; (2) and *Venimus adorare*, the end of their coming. But for the better conceiving it I will take another course, to set forth these points to be handled.

Their faith first: faith – in that they never ask 'Whether He be', but 'Where He is born'; for that born He is, that they stedfastly believe.

Then 'the work or service' of this faith, as St Paul calleth it; 'the touch or trial', as St Peter; the *ostende mihi*, as St James; of this their faith in these five.

1. Their confessing of it in *venerunt dicentes*. *Venerunt*; they were no sooner come, but *dicentes*, they tell it out; confess Him and His birth to be the cause of their coming.
2. Secondly, as confess their faith, so the ground of their faith; *vidimus enim*, for they had 'seen' His star; and His star being risen, by it they knew He must be risen too.
3. Thirdly, as St Paul calls them in Abraham's, *vestigia fidei*, 'the steps of their faith', in *venimus*, 'their coming' – coming such a journey, at such a time, with such speed.
4. Fourthly, when they were come, their diligent enquiring Him out by *ubi est?* for here is the place of it, asking after Him to find where He was.
5. And last, when they had found Him, the end of their seeing, coming, seeking; and all for no other end but to worship Him. Here they say it, at the eleventh verse they do it in these two acts: *procidentes*, their 'falling down', and *obtulerunt*, their 'offering' to Him. Worship Him with their bodies, worship Him with their goods; their worship and ours the true worship of Christ.

★   ★   ★

The text is of a star, and we may make all run on a star, that so the text and day may be suitable, and Heaven and earth hold a correspondence. St Peter calls faith 'the day-star rising in our hearts', which sorts well with the star in the text rising in the sky. That in the sky manifesting itself from above to them; this in their hearts manifesting itself from below to Him, to Christ. Manifesting itself by these five:

1. by *ore fit confessio*, 'the confessing of it';
2. by *fides est substantia*, 'the ground of it';
3. by *vestigia fidei*, 'the steps of it' in their painful coming;
4. by their *ubi est?* 'careful enquiring';
5. and last, by *adorare Eum*, 'their devout worshipping'.

These five, as so many beams of faith, the day-star risen in their hearts. To take notice of them. For every one of them is of the nature of a condition, so as if we fail in them, *non lucet nobis stella haec*, 'we have no part in the light, or conduct of this star'. Neither in *stellam*, 'the star itself', nor in *Eius*, 'in Him Whose the star is' that is, not in Christ neither.

★   ★   ★

We have now got us a star on earth for that in Heaven, and these both lead us to a third. So as upon the matter three stars we have, and each his proper manifestation.

1. The first in the firmament; that appeared unto them, and in them to us – a figure of St Paul's 'grace of God appearing, and bringing salvation to all men', Jews and Gentiles and all.
2. The second here on earth is St Peter's *Lucifer in cordibus*, and this appeared in them, and so must in us. Appeared (1) in their eyes – *vidimus*; (2) in their feet – *venimus*; (3) in their lips – *dicentes ubi est*; (4) in their knees – *procidentes* 'falling down'; (5) in their hands – *obtulerunt* 'by offering'.' These five every one a beam of this star.

3. The third in Christ Himself, St John's star. 'The generation and root of David, the bright morning Star, Christ.' And He, His double appearing: One at this time now, when He appeared in great humility; and we see and come to Him by faith. The other, which we wait for, even 'the blessed hope, and appearing of the great God and our Saviour' in the majesty of His glory.

These three: (1) The first that manifested Christ to them; (2) The second that manifested them to Christ; (3) The third Christ Himself, in Whom both these were as it were in conjunction. Christ 'the bright morning Star' of that day which shall have no night; the *beatifica visio*, 'the blessed sight' of which day is the *consummatum est* of our hope and happiness for ever.

Of these three stars the first is gone, the third yet to come, the second only is present. We to look to that, and to the five beams of it. That is, it must do us all the good, and bring us to the third.

St Luke calleth faith the 'door of faith'. At this door let us enter. Here is a coming, and 'he that cometh to God' must 'believe that Christ is'; so do these. They never ask *an sit* but *ubi sit?* Not 'whether' but 'where He is born'. They that ask *ubi Qui natus?* take *natus* for granted, presuppose that born He is. Herein is faith – faith of Christ's being born, the third article of the Christian Creed.

★   ★   ★

And what believe they of Him? Out of their own words here:

1. First, that *natus*, that 'born' He is, and so Man He is – His human nature.
2. And as His nature, so His office, in *natus est Rex*, 'born a King'. They believe that too.
3. But *Judaeorum* may seem to be a bar; for then, what have they to do with 'the King of the Jews'? They be Gentiles, none of His lieges, no relation to Him at all. What do they, seeking or

worshipping Him? But weigh it well, and it is no bar. For this they seem to believe: He is so *Rex Judaeorum*, 'King of the Jews', as He is *adorandus a Gentibus*, 'the Gentiles to adore Him'. And though born in Jewry, yet Whose birth concerned them though Gentiles, though born far off in the 'mountains of the East'. They to have some benefit by Him and His birth, and for that to do Him worship, seeing *officium fundatur in beneficio* ever.

4. As thus born in earth, so a star He hath in Heaven of His own – *stellam Eius*, 'His star'; He the owner of it. Now we know the stars are the stars of Heaven, and He that Lord of them Lord of Heaven too; and so to be adored to them, of us, and of all. St John puts them together: 'the root and generation of David', His earthly; and 'the bright morning star', His Heavenly or Divine generation. *Haec est fides Magorum*, this is the mystery of their faith. In *natus est*, man; in *stellam Eius*, God. In *Rex*, 'a King', though of the Jews, yet the good of Whose Kingdom should extend and stretch itself far and wide to Gentiles and all; and He of all to be adored. This, for *corde creditur*, the day-star itself in their hearts. Now to the beams of this star.

Next to *corde creditur* is *ore fit confessio*, 'the confession' of this faith. It is in *venerunt dicentes*, they came with it in their mouths. *Venerunt*, they were no sooner come, but they spake of it so freely, to so many, as it came to Herod's ear and troubled him not a little that any King of the Jews should be worshipped beside himself. So then their faith is no bosom-faith, kept to themselves without ever a *dicentes*, without saying any thing of it to anybody. No; *credidi, propter quod locutus sum*, 'they believed, and therefore they spake'.

The star in their hearts cast one beam out at their mouths. And though Herod who was but *Rex factus* could evil brook to hear of *Rex natus* – must needs be offended at it, yet they were not afraid to say it. And though they came from the East, those parts to whom and their King the Jews had long time been captives and their underlings, they were not ashamed neither to tell, that One of the Jew's race they came to seek; and to seek Him to the end 'to worship Him'. So neither afraid of Herod, nor ashamed of Christ; but professed their errand, and cared not who knew it. This for their confessing Him boldly.

But faith is said by the Apostle to be *hypostasis*, and so there is a good 'ground'; and *elenchos*, and so hath a good 'reason' for it. This puts the difference between *fidelis* and *credulus* (or as Solomon terms him *fatuus, qui credit omni verbo*); between faith and lightness of belief. Faith hath ever a ground; *vidimus enim* – an *enim*, a reason for it, and is ready to render it. How came you to believe? *Audivimus enim*, 'for we have heard an Angel', say the shepherds. *Vidimus enim*, 'for we have seen a star' say the Magi, and this is a well-grounded faith. We came not of our heads, we came not before we saw some reason for it – saw that which set us on coming; *Vidimus enim stellam Eius.*

★   ★   ★

Vidimus stellam – we can well conceive that; any that will but look up, may see a star. But how could they see the *Eius* of it, that it was His? Either that it belonged to any, or that He it was it belonged to. This passeth all perspective; no astronomy could show them this. What by course of nature the stars can produce, that they by course of art or observation may discover. But this birth was above nature. No trigon, triplicity, exaltation could bring it forth. They are but idle that set figures for it. The star should not have been His, but He the star's, if it had gone that way. Some other light then, they saw this *Eius* by.

Now with us in Divinity there be but two in all: (1) *Vespertina* and (2) *Matutina lux*. *Vespertina*, 'the owl-light' of our reason or skill is too dim to see it by. No remedy then but it must be as Esay [Isaiah] calls it, *matutina lux*, 'the morning-light', the light of God's law must certify them of the *Eius* of it. There, or not at all to be had whom this star did portend.

And in the Law, there we find it in the twenty-fourth [chapter] of Numbers. One of their own Prophets that came from whence they came, 'from the mountains of the East', was ravished in spirit, 'fell in a trance, had his eyes opened', and saw the *Eius* of it many an hundred years before it rose. Saw *orietur in Jacob*, that there it should 'rise', which is as much as *natus est* here. Saw *stella*, that He should be 'the bright morning-Star', and so might well have a star to represent Him. Saw *sceptrum in Israel*, which is just as much as *Rex Judaeorum*, that it should portend a King there – such a King as should not only 'smite the corners of Moab', that is Balak their enemy for the present; but 'should reduce and bring under Him all the sons of Seth', that is all the world; for all are now Seth's sons, Caine's were all drowned in the flood. Here now is the *Eius* of it clear. A Prophet's eye might discern this; never a Chaldean of them all could take it with his astrolabe. Balaam's eyes were opened to see it, and he helped to open their eyes by leaving behind him this prophecy to direct them how to apply it, when it should arise to the right *Eius* of it.

But these had not the law. It is hard to say that the Chaldee paraphrase was extant long before this. They might have had it. Say, they had it not: if Moses were so careful to record this prophecy in his book, it may well be thought that some memory of this so memorable a prediction was left remaining among them of the East, his own country where he was born and brought up. And some help they might have from Daniel too, who lived all his time in Chaldea and Persia, and prophesied among them of such a King, and set the just time of it.

And this, as it is conceived, put the difference between the East and the West. For I ask, was it *vidimus in Oriente* with them? Was it not *vidimus in Occidente*? In the West such a star – it or the fellow of it was seen nigh about that time, or the Roman stories deceive us. Toward the end of Augustus' reign such a star was seen, and much scanning there was about it. Pliny saith it was generally holden, that star to be *faustum sydus*, 'a lucky comet', and portended good to the world, which few or no comets do. And Virgil, who then lived, would needs take upon him to set down the *eius* of it – *Ecce Dionaei etc* entitled Caesar to it. And verily there is no man that can without admiration read his sixth Eclogue, of a birth that time expected, that should be the offspring of the gods, and that should take away their sins. Whereupon it hath gone for current – the East and West, *Vidimus* both.

But by the light of their prophecy, the East they went straight to the right *Eius*. And for want for this light the West wandered, and gave it a wrong *eius*; as Virgil, applying it to little Salonine: and as evil hap was, while he was making his verses, the poor child died; and so his star shot, vanished, and came to nothing. Their *vidimus* never came to a *venimus*; they neither went, nor worshipped Him as these here did.

But by this we see, when all is done, thither we must come for our morning light; to this book, to the word of prophecy. All our *vidimus stellam* is as good as nothing without it. That star is past and gone, long since; 'Heaven and earth shall pass, but this world shall not pass.' Here on this, we to fix our eye and to ground our faith. Having this, though we neither hear Angel nor see star, we may by the grace of God do fully well. For even they that have had both those, have been fain to resolve into this as their last, best, and chiefest point of all. Witness St Peter: he, saith he, and they with him, 'saw Christ's glory, and heard the voice from Heaven in the Holy Mount'. What then? After both these, *audivimus* and *vidimus*, both senses, he comes to this, *Habemus autem firmiorem etc.* 'We have a more sure word of prophecy' than both these; *firmiorem*, a 'more sure', a more clear, than them both. And *si hic legimus* – for *legimus* is *vidimus* – 'if here we read it written', it is enough to ground our faith, and let the star go.

And yet, to end this point: both these, the star and the prophecy, they are but *circumfusa lux* – without both. Besides these there must be a light within in the eye; else, we know, for all them nothing will be seen. And that must come from Him, and the enlightening of His Spirit. Take this for a rule: no knowing of *Eius absque Eo*, 'of His without Him', whose it is. Neither of the star, without Him That created it; nor of the prophecy, without Him That inspired it. But this third coming too; He sending the light of His Spirit within into their minds, they then saw clearly, this the star, now the time. He the Child That this day was born.

He That sent these two without, sent also this third within, and then it was *vidimus* indeed. The light of the star in their eyes, the 'word of prophecy' in their ears, the beam of His Spirit in their hearts; these three made up a full *vidimus*. And so much for *vidimus stellam Eius*, the occasion of their coming.

★   ★   ★

Now to *venimus*, their coming itself. And it follows well. For it is not a star only, but a load-star; and whither should *stella Eius ducere*, but *ad Eum*? 'Whither lead us, but to Him Whose the star is?' – the star to the star's Master.

All this while we have been at *dicentes*, 'saying' and seeing; now we shall come to *facientes*, see them do somewhat upon it. It is not saying nor seeing will serve St James; he will call, and be still calling for *ostende mihi*, 'shew me thy faith by some work'. And well may he be allowed to call for it this day; it is the day of *vidimus*, appearing, being seen. You have seen His star, let Him now see your star another while. And so they do. Make your faith to be seen; so it is – their faith in the steps of their faith. And so was Abraham's first by coming forth of his country; as these here do, and so 'walk in the steps of the faith of Abraham', do his first work.

It is not commended to stand 'gazing up into Heaven' too long; not on Christ Himself ascending, much less on His star. For they sat not still gazing on the star. Their *vidimus* begat *venimus*; their seeing made them come, come a great journey. *Venimus* is soon said, but a short word; but many a wide and weary step they made before they could come to say *Venimus*, Lo, here 'we are come'; come, and at our journey's end. To look a little on it. In this their coming we consider:

1. First, the distance of the place they came from. It was not hard by as the shepherds – but a step to Bethlehem over the fields; this was riding many a hundred miles, and cost them many a day's journey.
2. Secondly, we consider the way that they came, if it be pleasant,

or plain and easy; for if it be, it is so much the better. This was nothing pleasant, for through deserts, all the way waste and desolate. Nor easy neither; for over the rocks and crags of both Arabias, specially Petraea, their journey lay.

3. Yet if safe – but it was not, but exceeding dangerous, as lying through the midst of the 'black tents of Kedar', a nation of thieves and cut-throats; to pass over the hills of robbers, infamous then, and infamous to this day. No passing without great troop or convoy.

4. Last we consider the time of their coming, the season of the year. It was no summer progress. A cold coming they had of it at this time of the year, just the worst time of the year to take a journey, and specially a long journey in. The ways deep, the weather sharp, the days short, the sun farthest off, in *solstitio brumali*, 'the very dead of winter'. *Venimus*, 'we are come' – if that be one *venimus*, 'we are now come', come at this time, that sure is another.

And these difficulties they overcame, of a wearisome, irksome, troublesome, dangerous, unseasonable journey; and for all this they came. And came it cheerfully and quickly, as appeareth by the speed they made. It was but *vidimus, venimus*, with them; 'they saw', and 'they came'; no sooner saw, but they set out presently. So as upon the first appearing of the star (as it might be last night), they knew it was Balaam's star; it called them away, they made ready straight to begin their journey this morning. A sign they were highly conceited of His birth, believed some great matter of it, that they took all these pains, made all this haste that they might be there to worship Him with all the possible speed they could. Sorry for nothing so much as that they could not be there soon enough, with the very first, to do it even this day, the day of His birth. All considered, there is more in *venimus* than shews at the first sight. It was not for nothing it was said in the first verse, *ecce venerunt*; their coming hath an *ecce* on it, it well deserves it.

And we, what should we have done? Sure these men of the East shall rise in judgement against the men of the West, that is us, and their faith against ours in this point. With them it was but *vidimus*, *venimus*; with us it would have been but *veniemus* at most. Our fashion is to see and see again before we stir a foot, specially if it be to the worship of Christ. Come such a journey at such a time? No; but fairly have put it off to the spring of the year, till the days longer, and the ways fairer, and the weather warmer, till better travelling to Christ. Our Epiphany would sure have fallen in Easter week at the soonest.

But then for the distance, desolateness, tediousness, and the rest, any of them were enough to mar our *venimus* quite. It must be no great way, first, we must come; we love not that. Well fare the shepherds, yet they came but hard by; rather like them than the Magi. Nay, not like them neither. For with us the nearer, lightly the farther off; our proverb is you know, 'The nearer the Church, the farther from God.'

Nor it must not be through no desert, over no Petraea. If rugged or uneven the way, if the weather ill-disposed, if any never so little danger, it is enough to stay us. To Christ we cannot travel, but weather and way and all must be fair. If not, no journey, but sit still and see farther. As indeed, all our religion is rather *vidimus*, a contemplation, than *venimus*, a motion, or stirring to do ought.

But when we do it, we must be allowed leisure. Ever *veniemus*, never *venimus*; ever coming, never come. We love to make no very great haste. To other things perhaps not to *adorare*, the place of the worship of God. Why should we? Christ is no wild-cat. What talk ye of twelve days? And if it be forty days hence, ye shall be sure to find His Mother and Him; she cannot be churched till then. What needs such haste? The truth is, we conceit Him and His birth but slenderly, and our haste is even thereafter. But if we be at that point, we must be out of this *venimus;* they like enough to leave us behind. Best get us a new Christmas in September; we are not like to come to Christ at this feast . . .

Morning prayer

Glory be to thee, Lord, glory be to thee.
Glory be to him that hath granted me sleep: for repose of
weakness, and for relief of the toils of this travailing flesh.

1. To enter on this and every day a perfect, holy, peaceful, health-
   ful, sinless day,
   Let us ask of the Lord.   *Grant it, O Lord.*

2. An angel of peace, a faithful guide, a guardian of our souls and
   bodies, tarrying round about me, and suggesting to me always
   what things are wholesome,
   Let us ask of the Lord.   *Grant it, O Lord.*

3. The forgiveness and the remission of all our sins, and of all our
   offences,
   Let us ask of the Lord.   *Grant it, O Lord.*

4. What things are good and expedient for our souls, and peace
   for the world,
   Let us ask of the Lord.   *Grant it, O Lord.*

5. To accomplish the residue of our lifetime in repentance and
   godly fear, in health and peace,
   Let us ask of the Lord.   *Grant it, O Lord.*

6. Whatsoever things are true, whatsoever things are honest,
   whatsoever things are just, whatsoever things are pure, what
   soever things are lovely, whatsoever things are of good report,
   if there be any virtue and if there be any praise, that we may
   think on these things and practise these things,
   Let us ask of the Lord.   *Grant it, O Lord.*

7. That the end of our life be Christian, sinless, shameless, and (if it like thee) painless, and a good defence at the appalling and fearful judgement-seat of Jesus Christ our Lord,
Let us ask of the Lord.   *Grant it, O Lord.*

Lancelot Andrewes

John Donne

To read a sermon by Donne (1572–1631) is like swiming in a warm, moving sea. He has an extraordinary mental control of his subject and sources. Every now and then an unexpected insight is presented in an arresting figure of speech. To our age he enjoys a high reputation of a poet, and a love poet at that. He had jettisoned a career in the law for the sake of marriage; he had jettisoned the Roman Catholic faith in favour of the established Church of England, and he then developed a sharp and burning public attitude to God reflected in his sermons as Dean of St Paul's in the last ten years of his life. Early editions of his 154 or so printed sermons are much sought after but there is surprisingly no full and cheap edition of them in print today.

A sermon preached at St Paul's upon Whitsunday 1629

And the Spirit of God moved upon the face of the waters. (Genesis 1:2)

The Church of God celebrates this day the third Person of the Holy, Blessed, and Glorious Trinity, the Holy Ghost. The Holy Ghost is the God, the Spirit of comfort; A Comforter; not one amongst others, but the comforter; not the principall, but the intire, the onely Comforter; and more than all that, the Comfort it selfe.

That is an attribute of the Holy Ghost, Comfort; And then the office of the Holy Ghost is to gather, to establish, to illumine, to governe that Church which the Son of God, from whom together with the Father, the Holy Ghost proceeds, hath purchased with his blood. So that, as the Holy Ghost is the Comforter, so is this Comfort exhibited by him to us, and exercised by him upon us, and does governe us, as members of that body of which Christ Jesus is the Head; that he hath brought us, and bred us, and fed us with the meanes of salvation, in his application of the merits of Christ to our soules, in the Ordinances of the Church.

In this Text is the first mention of this Third Person of the Trinity; And it is the first mention of any distinct Person in the God-head; In the first verse, there is an intimation of the Trinity, in that *Bara Elohim*, that *Gods*, Gods in the plurall are said to have made heaven, and earth.

And then, as the Church after having celebrated the memory of All Saints, together in that one day, which we call All Saints day, begins in the celebration of particular Saints, first with Saint Andrew, who first of any applied himself to Christ out of Saint John Baptists Schoole after Christs Baptisme; so Moses having given us an intimation of God, and the three Persons altogether in that *Bara Elohim* before, gives us first notice of this Person, the Holy Ghost, in particular, because he applies to us the Mercies of the Father, and the Merits of the son, and moves upon the face of the waters, and actuates, and fecundates our soules, and generates that knowledge, and that comfort, which we have in the knowledge of God.

Now the moving of the Holy Ghost upon the face of the waters in this Text, cannot be literally understood of his working upon man; for man was not yet made; but when man is made, that is, made the man of God in Christ; there in that new Creation the Holy Ghost begins again, with a new moving upon the face of the waters in the Sacrament of Baptisme, which is the Conception of a Christian in the wombe of the Church.

Therefore we shall consider these words: 'And the Spirit of God moved upon the face of the waters'; first, literally in the first, and then spiritually in the second Creation; first how the Holy Ghost moved upon the face of the Waters in making this world for us, And then how he moves upon the face of the Waters againe, in making us for the other world. In which two severall parts we shall consider these three termes in our Text, both in the Macrocosme, and Microcosme, the Great and the Lesser world, man extended in the world, and the world contracted, and abridged into man; first, *Quid Spiritus Dei?* What this Power, or this Person, which is here called the Spirit of God, is, for whether it be a Power, or a Person, hath been diversly disputed; And secondly,

Quid ferebatur? What this Action, which is here called a Moving, was; for whether a Motion, or a Rest, an Agitation, or an Incubation, of that Power, or that Person, hath been disputed too; And lastly, *Quid super faciem aquarum?* What the subject of this Action, the face of the waters, was; for, whether it were a stirring, and an awakening of a power that was naturally in those waters, to produce creatures, or whether it were an infusing a new power, which till then those waters had not, hath likewise beene disputed, And in these three, the Person, the Action, the Subject, considered twice over, in the Creation first, and in our regeneration in the Christian Church after, we shall determine all that is necessary for the literall, and for the spirituall sense of these words, 'And the Spirit of God moved upon the face of the waters.'

★   ★   ★

First then, undertaking the consideration of the literall sense, and after, of the spirituall, we joyne with St Augustine, *Sint castae deliciae meae Scripturae tuae*; Lord I love to be conversant in thy Scriptures, let my conversation with thy Scriptures be a chast conversation; that I discover no nakednesse therein; offer not to touch any thing in thy Scriptures, but that that thou hast vouchsafed to unmask, and manifest unto me: *Nec fallar in eis, nec fallam ex eis*; Lord, let not me mistake the meaning of thy Scriptures, nor mislead others, by imputing a false sense to them. *Non frustra scribuntur*, sayes he; Lord, thou hast writ nothing to no purpose; thou wouldst be understood in all: But not in all, by all men, at all times; *Confiteor tibi quicquid invenero in libris tuis*; Lord, I acknowledge that I receive from thee, whatsoever I understand in thy word; for else I doe not understand it. Thus that blessed Father meditates upon the word of God; he speakes of this beginning of the Book of Genesis; and he speaks lamenting, *Scripsit Moses et abiit*, a little Moses hath said, and alas he is gone; *Si hic esset, tenerem eum, et per te rogarem*, If Moses were here, I would hold him here, and begge of him, for thy sake to tell me thy meaning in his words, of this Creation. But sayes he, since I cannot speake with Moses,

Te, quo plenus vera dixit, Veritas, rogo, I begge of thee who are Truth itselfe, as thou enabledst him to utter it, enable me to understand what he hath said. So difficult a thing seemed it to that intelligent Father, to understand this history, this mystery of the Creation. But yet though he found that divers senses offered themselves, he did not doubt of finding the Truth: For, *Deus meus lumen oculorum meorum in occulto,* sayes he, O my God, the light of mine eyes, in this dark inquisition, since divers senses, arise out of these words, and all true, *Quid mihi obest, si aliud ego sensero, quam sensit alius, eum sensisse, qui scripsit?* What hurt followes, though I follow another sense, then some other man takes to be Moses sense? For his may be a true sense, and so may mine, and neither be Moses his. Hee passes from prayer, and protestation, to counsell, and direction; *In diversitate sententiarum verarum, concordiam pariat ipsa veritas,* Where divers senses arise, and all true, (that is, that none of them oppose the truth) let truth agree them. But what is Truth? God; And what is God? Charity; Therefore let Charity reconcile such differences. *Legitime lege utamur,* sayes he, let us use the Law lawfully; Let us use our liberty of reading Scriptures according to the Law of liberty; that is, charitably to leave others to their liberty, if they but differ from us, and not differ from Fundamentall Truths.

Si quis quaerat ex me, quid horum Moses senserit, If any man ask me, which of these, which may be all true, Moses meant, *Non sunt sermones isti confessiones,* Lord, sayes hee, This that I say is not said by way of Confession, as I intend it should, if I doe not freely confesse, that I cannot tell, which Moses meant; But yet I can tell, that this that I take to be his meaning is true; and that is enough. Let him that findes a true sense of any place, rejoyce in it, Let him that does not beg it of thee, *Utquid mihi molestus est?* Why should any man presse me, to give him the true sense of Moses here, or of the holy Ghost, in any darke place of Scripture? *Ego illuminen ullum hominem, venientem in mundum?* sayes he; Is that said of me, that I am the light, that enlightned every man, any man, that comes into this world? So far I will goe, sayes he, so far will we, in his modesty and humility accompany him, as still to propose,

63

Quod luce veritatis, quod fruge utilitatis excellit, such a sense as agrees with other Truths, that are evident in other places of Scripture, and such a sense as may conduce most to edification.

For to those two, does that heavenly Father reduce the foure Elements, that make up a right exposition of Scripture; which are, first, the glory of God, such a sense as may most advance it; secondly, the analogie of faith, such a sense as may violate no confessed Article of Religion; and thirdly, exaltation of devotion, such a sense, as may carry us most powerfully upon the apprehension of the next life; and lastly, extension of charity, such a sense as may best hold us in peace, or reconcile us, if we differ from one another. And within these limits wee shall containe our selves: The glory of God, the analogie of faith, the exaltation of devotion, the extension of charity. In all the rest, that belongs to the explication or application, to the literall, or spirituall sense of these words, 'And the Spirit of God moved upon the face of the waters', to which having stopped a little upon this generall consideration, the exposition of darke places, we passe now.

Within these rules we proceed to enquire, who this Spirit of God is, or what it is; whether a Power, or a Person. The Jews who are afraid of the Truth, lest they should meete evidences of the doctrine of the Trinity, and so of the Messias, the Son of God, if they should admit any spirituall sense, admit none, but cleave so close to the letter, as that to them the Scripture becomes *Litera occidens,* A killing Letter, and the savour of death unto death. They therefore, in this Spirit of God, are so far from admitting any Person, that is, God, as they admit no extraordinary operation, or vertue proceeding from God in this place; but they take the word here (as in many other places of Scripture it does) to signifie onely a winde, and then that that addition of the name of God (The Spirit of God) which is in their Language a denotation of a vehemency, of a high degree, of a superlative, (as when it is said of Saul, *Sopor Domini,* A sleepe of God was upon him, it is intended of a deepe, a dead sleepe) inforces, induces no more but that a very strong winde blew upon the face of the waters, and so in a great part dryed them up.

And this opinion I should let flye away with the winde, if onely the Jews had said it. But Theodoret hath said it too, and therefore we afford it so much answer, That it is a strange anticipation, that Winde – which is a mixt Meteor to the making whereof divers occasions concurre with exhalations – should be thus imagined, before any of these causes of Winds were created, or produced, and that there should be an effect before a cause, is somewhat irregular. In Lapland, the Witches are said to sell winds to all passengers; but that is but to turne those windes that Nature does produce, which way they will; but in our case, the Jews, and they that follow them, dreame winds, before any winds, or cause of winds was created; The Spirit of God here cannot be the Wind.

It cannot be that neither, which some great men in the Christian Church have imagined it to be: *Operatio Dei*, The power of God working upon the waters, (so some) or, *Efficientia Dei*, A power by God infused into the waters; so others. And to that St Augustine comes so neare, as to say once in the negative, *Spiritus Dei hic, res dei est, sed non ipse Deus est*, The Spirit of God in this place is something proceeding from God, but it is not God himselfe; And once in the affirmative, *Posse esse vitalem creaturam, qua universus mundus movetur*, That this Spirit of God may be that universall power, which sustaines, and inanimates the whole world, which the Platoniques have called the Soule of the world, and others intend by the name of Nature, and we doe well, if we call The providence of God.

But there is more of God in this Action then the Instrument of God, Nature, or the Vice-roy of God, Providence; for as the person of God, the Son was in the Incarnation, so the person of God, the Holy Ghost was in this Action; though far from that manner of becomming one and the same thing with the waters, which was done in the Incarnation of Christ, who became therein perfect man. That this word the Spirit of God, is intended of the Person of the Holy Ghost in other places of Scripture is evident, undeniable, unquestionable, and that therefore it may be so taken here. Where it is said, 'The Spirit of God shall rest upon him', (upon the Messiah), where it is said by himselfe, 'The Lord and his

Spirit is upon me', And, 'the Lord and his Spirit hath anointed me', there it is certainly, and therefore here it may be probably spoken of the Holy Ghost personally. It is no impossible sense, it implies no contradiction; It is no inconvenient sense, it offends no other article; it is no new sense; nor can we assigne any time when it was a new sense: The eldest Fathers adhere to it, as the ancientest interpretation.

Saint Basil saies not onely, *Constantissime asseverandum est*, We must constantly maintaine that interpretation, (for all that might be his owne opinion) not onely therefore, *Quia verius est*, (for that might be, but because he found it to be the common opinion of those times) but *Quia a majoribus nostris approbatum*, because it is accepted for the true sense, by the Ancients; The Ancients, saies that ancient Father Basil; which reason prevailes upon St Ambrose too, *Nos cum sanctorum, et fidelium sententia congruentes*, We beleeve, and beleeve it because the Ancients beleeved it to be so, that this is spoken generally of the Holy Ghost. St Basil and St Ambrose assume it, as granted, St Hierom disputes it, argues, concludes it, *Vivificator, ergo Conditor, ergo Deus*; This Spirit of God gave life, therefore this Spirit was a Creator; therefore God. St Augustine prints his seale deepe; *Secundum quod ego intelligere possum, ita est*, as far as my understanding can reach, it is so; and his understanding reached far. But he addes, *Nec ullo modo*, etc, Neither can it possibly be otherwise.

We cannot tell, whether that Poem which is called Genesis, be Tertullians, or Cyprians; It hath beene thought an honour to the learnedest of the Fathers, to have beene the Author of a good Poem; In that Poem this text is paraphrased thus, *Immensusque Deus super aequora vasta meabat*; God, God personally moved upon the waters. Truly the later Schoole is (as they have used it) a more Poeticall part of divinity, then any of the Poems of the Fathers are, (take in Lactantius his *Poem of the Phoenix*, and all the rest) and for the Schoole, there Aquinas saies, *Secundum Sanctos, intelligimus Spiritum sanctum*, As the holy Fathers have done, we also understand this personally of the Holy Ghost.

To end this, these words doe not afford such an argument for the Trinity, or the third Person thereof, the Holy Ghost, as is strong enough to convert, or convince a Jew, because it may have another sense; but we, who by Gods abundant goodnesse have otherwise an assurance, and faith in this doctrine, acknowledge all those other places, 'Thou sendest forth thy Spirit, and they are created, By his Spirit he hath garnished the Heavens', and the rest of that kinde, to be all but ecchoes from this voyce, returnes for Iob, and from David, and the rest of this doctrine of all comfort, first, and betimes delivered from Moses, that there is a distinct person in the Godhead, whose attribute is goodnesse, whose office is application, whose way is comfort. And so we passe from our first, That it is not onely the Power of God, but the Person of God, To the second, in this branch, His Action, *Ferebatur.*

The Action of the Spirit of God, the Holy Ghost, in this place, is expressed in a word, of a double and very diverse signification; for it signifies motion and it signifies rest. And therefore, as St Augustine argues upon those words of David, 'Thou knewest my downe sitting, and my uprising', That God knew all that he did, betweene his downe sitting and his uprising; So in this word which signifies the Holy Ghosts first motion, and his last rest, we comprehend all that was done in the production, and creation of the Creatures. This word, we translate, 'As the Eagle fluttereth over her young ones, so it is a word of Motion'; And St Hierom upon our Text expresses it by *Incubabat*, to sit upon her young ones, to hatch them, or to preserve them, so it is a word of rest. And so, the Jews take this word to signifie, properly the birds hatching of eggs. St Cyprian unites the two significations well, *Spiritus sanctus dabat aquis motum et limitem*; The Holy Ghost enabled the waters to move, and appointed how, and how far they should move. The beginnings, and the waies, and the ends, must proceed from God, and from God the Holy Ghost: That is, by those meanes, and those declarations, by which God doth manifest himselfe to us, for that is the office of the Holy Ghost, to manifest and apply God to us. Now the word in our Text is not truly *Ferebatur*, The Spirit moved, which denotes a thing past; but the word is *Movens*, Moving, a Participle of the present; So that we ascribe first God's manifestation of himself in the creation, and then the continuall manifestation of himself in his providence, to the Holy Ghost; for God had two purposes in the creation, *Ut sint, ut maneant*, That the creature should be, and be still; That it should exist at first, and subsist after; Be made, and made permanent. God did not mean that Paradise should have been of so small use when he made it; he made it for a perpetuall habitation for man. God did not mean that man should be the subject of his wrath when he made him; he made him to take pleasure in, and to shed glory upon him. The Holy Ghost moves, he is the first author; the Holy Ghost perpetuates, settles, establishes, he is our rest, and acquiescence, and centre; Beginning, Way, End, all is in this word, *Recaph*; The Spirit of God moved, and rested. And upon what? 'And the Spirit of God moved upon the face of the waters.'

St Augustine observing aright, That at this time, of which this Text is spoken, The waters enwrapped all the whole substance, the whole matter, of which all things were to be created, all was surrounded with the waters, all was embowelled, and enwombed in the waters; And so the Holy Ghost moving, and resting upon the face of the waters, moved, and rested, did his office upon the whole Masse of the world, and so produced all that was produced; and this admits no contradiction, no doubt, but that thus the thing was done, and that this, this word implies. But whether the Holy Ghost wrought this production of the severall creatures, by himself, or whether he infused, and imprinted a naturall power in the waters, and all the substance under the waters, to produce creatures naturally of themselves, hath received some doubt. It need not: for the worke ascribed to the Holy Ghost here is not the working by nature, but the creating of nature; Not what nature did after, but how nature herself was created at first. In this action, this moving, and resting upon the face of the waters (that is, all involved in the waters) the Spirit of God, the Holy Ghost, hatched, produced then all those creatures; For no power infused into the waters, or earth then, could have enabled that earth, then to have produced Trees with ripe fruits, in an instant, nor the waters to have brought forth Whales, in their growth, in an instant. The Spirit of God produced them then, and established and conserves ever since, that seminall power which we call Nature, to produce all creatures (then first made by himselfe) in a perpetuall Succession.

And so have you these words, 'And the Spirit of God moved upon the face of the waters', literally, historically: And now these three termes, 'The Spirit of God, Moved, Upon the face of the waters', You are also to receive in a spirituall sense, in the second world, the Christian Church: The Person, the Action, the Subject, the holy Ghost, and him moving, and moving upon the waters, in our regeneration.

Here, as before, our first Terme, and Consideration, is the name, The Spirit of God; And here God knows, we know too many, even amongst the outward professors of the Christian religion, that in this name, The Spirit of God, take knowledge only of a power of God, and not of a person of God: They say it is the working of God, but not God working. *Mira profunditas eloquiorum tuorum*; The waters in the creation, were not so deep as the word of God, that delivers that creation. *Ecce, ante nos superficies blandiens pueris*, sayes that Father; We, we that are but babes in understanding, as long as we are but naturall men, see the superficies, the top, the face, the outside of these waters, *Sed mira profunditas, Deus meus, mira profunditas*, But it is an infinite depth, Lord my God, an infinite depth to come to the bottome. The bottome is, to professe, and to feele the distinct working of the three distinct persons of the Trinity, Father, Son, and holy Ghost. *Rara anima, qua cum de illa loquitur, sciat quid loquatur*, Not one man, not one Christian amongst a thousand, who when he speaks of the Trinity, knows what he himself meanes. Naturall men will write of lands of Pygmies, and of lands of Giants; and write of Phoenixes, and of Unicornes; But yet advisedly they do not beleeve, (at least confidently they do not know) that there are such Giants, or such Pygmies, such Unicorns or Phoenixes in the world. Christians speak continually of the Trinity, and the Holy Ghost, but alas, advisedly, they know not what they mean in those names. The most know nothing, for want of consideration; They that have considered it enough, and spent thoughts enough upon the Trinity, to know as much as needs be known thereof, *Contendunt et dimicant, et nemo sine pace videt istam visionem*, They dispute, and they wrangle, and they scratch, and wound one another's reputations, and they assist the common enemy of Christianity by their uncharitable differences, *Et sine pace*. And without peace, and mildnesse, and love, and charity, no man comes to know the holy Ghost, who is the God of peace, and the God of love. *Da quod amo; amo enim, nam et hoc tu dedisti*; I am loath to part from this father, and he is loath to be parted from, for he sayes this in more than one place; Lord thou hast enamoured mee, made me in love; let me enjoy that that I love; That is, the holy Ghost: That as I feele the power of God (which sense, is a gift of the Holy Ghost) I may without disputing rest in the beliefe of that person of the Trinity, that that Spirit of God, that moves upon these waters, is not only the power, but a person in the Godhead.

This is the person, without whom there is no Father, no Son of God to me, the holy Ghost. And his action, his operation is expressed in this word, *Ferebatur*, The Spirit of God moved; Which word, as before, is here also a comprehensive word, and denotes both motion, and rest; beginnings, and wayes, and ends. We may best consider the motion, the stirring of the Holy Ghost in zeale, and the rest of the Holy Ghost in moderation; If we be without zeale, we have not the motion; If we be without moderation, we have not the rest, the peace of the Holy Ghost. The moving of the Holy Ghost upon me, is, as the moving of the minde of an Artificer, upon that piece of work that is then under his hand. A Jeweller, if he would make a jewell to answer the form of any flower, or any other figure, his minde goes along with his hand, nay prevents his hand, and he thinks in himself, a Ruby will conduce best to the expressing of this and an Emeraud of this. The Holy Ghost undertakes every man amongst us, and would make every man fit for God's service, in some way, in some profession; and the Holy Ghost sees, that one man profits most by one way, another by another, and moves their zeal to pursue those wayes, and those meanes, by which, in a rectified conscience, they finde most profit. And except a man have this sense, what doth him most good, and a desire to pursue that, the Holy Ghost doth not move, not stir up a zeale in him.

But then if God do afford him the benefit of these his Ordinances, in a competent measure for him, and he will not be satisfied with Manna, but will needs have Quailes, that is, cannot make one meale of Prayers, except he have a Sermon, nor satisfied with his Gomer of Manna, (with those Prayers which are appointed in the Church) nor satisfied with those Quailes which God sends, (the preaching of solid and fundamental doctrines) but must have birds of Paradise, un-revealed mysteries out of God's own bosome preached unto him, howsoever the Holy Ghost may seem to have moved, yet he doth not rest upon him; and from the beginning the office and operation of the Holy Ghost was double; He moved, and rested upon the waters in the creation; he came, and tarried still upon Christ in his Baptisme: He moves us to a zeale of laying hold upon the meanes of salvation which God offers us in the Church; and he settles us in a peacefull conscience, that by having well used those meanes, we are made his. A holy hunger and thirst of the Word and Sacraments, a remorse, and compunction for former sins, a zeale to promote the cause, and glory of God, by word, and deed, this is the motion of the Holy Ghost: And then, to content my self with God's measure of temporall blessings, and for spirituall, that I do serve God faithfully in that calling which I lawfully professe, as far as that calling will admit, (for he, upon whose hand-labour the sustentation of his family depends, may offend God in running after many working dayes Sermons). This peace of conscience, this acquiescence of having done that that belongs to me, this is the rest of the Spirit of God. And this motion, and this rest is said to be done *Super faciem*, 'And the Spirit of God moved upon the face of the waters', which is our last consideration.

In the moving of the Spirit of God upon the waters, we told you before, it was disputed, whether the Holy Ghost did immediately and inanimate, and inable those substances, (the water, and all contained under the waters) to produce creatures in their divers specifications. In this moving of the Spirit of God upon the waters, in our regeneration, it hath also been much disputed, How the Holy Ghost works, in producing man's supernaturall actions; whether so immediately, as that it be altogether without dependance, or relation to any faculty in man, or man himselfe have some concurrence, and co-operation therein. There we found, that in the first creation, God wrought otherwise for the production of creatures, then he does not; At first he did it immediately, intirely, by himself; Now, he hath delegated, and substituted nature, and imprinted a naturall power in every thing to produce the like. So in the first act of man's Conversion, God may be conceived to work otherwise, then in his subsequent holy actions; for in the first, man cannot be conceived to doe any thing, in the rest he may: not that in the rest God does not all; but that God findes a better disposition, and souplenesse, and maturity, and mellowing, to concurre with his motion in that man, who hath formerly been accustomed to a sense, and good use of his former graces, then in him, who in his first conversion, receives, but then, the first motions of his grace.

But yet, even in the first creation, the Spirit of God did not move upon that nothing, which was before God made heaven and earth: But he moved upon the waters; though those waters had nothing in themselves, to answer his motion, yet he had waters to move upon: Though our faculties have nothing in themselves to answer the motions of the Spirit of God, yet upon our faculties the Spirit of God works; And as out of those waters, those creatures did proceed, though not from those waters, so out of our faculties the Spirit of God works; And as out of those waters those creatures did proceed, though not from those waters, so out of our faculties, though not from our faculties, doe our good actions proceed too. All in all, is from the love of God; but there is something for God to love; There is a man, there is a soul in that man, there is a will in that soul; and God is in love with this man, and this soul, and this will, and would have it. *Non amor ita egenus & indigus, ut rebus quas diligit subjiciatur,* sayes St Augustine excellently: The love of God to us is not so poore a love, as our love to

72

one another; that his love to us should make him subject to us, as ours does to them whom we love; but *Superfertur*, sayes that Father, and our Text, he moves above us; He loves us, but with a Powerfull, a Majesticall, an Imperiall, a Commanding love; He offers those, whom he makes his, his grace; but so, as he sometimes will not be denied. So the Spirit moves spiritually upon the waters; He comes to the waters, to our naturall faculties; but he moves above those waters, He inclines, he governes, he commands those faculties; And this his motion, upon those waters, we may usefully consider, in some divers applications and assimilations of water, to man, and the divers uses there of towards man. We will name but a few; Baptisme, Sin, Tribulation, and Death, and we have done.

The water of Baptisme, is the water that runs through all the Fathers; All the Fathers that had occasion to dive, or dip in these waters (to say any thing of them) make these first waters, in the Creation, the figure of baptisme. Therefore Tertullian makes the water, *Primam sedem Spiritus Sancti*, The progresse, and the setled house, The voyage, and the harbour, The circumference, and the centre of the Holy Ghost: And therefore St Hierome calls these waters, *Matrem Mundi*, The Mother of the World; and this in the figure of Baptisme. *Nascentem Mundum in figura Baptismi parturiebat*, The waters brought forth the whole World, were delivered of the whole World, as a Mother is delivered of a childe; and this, *In figura Baptismi*, To fore-shew, that the waters also should bring forth the Church; That the Church of God should be borne of the Sacrament of Baptisme: So sayes Damascen, And he establishes it with better authority than his owne, *Hoc Divinus asseruit Basilius*, sayes he, This Divine Basil said, *Hoc factum, quia per Spiritum Sanctum, et aquam voluit renovare hominem*; The Spirit of God wrought upon the waters in the Creation, because he meant to doe so after, in the regeneration of man.

And therefore *Pristinam sedem recognoscens conquiescit*, Till the Holy Ghost have moved upon our children in Baptisme, let us not think all done, that belongs to those children; And when the Holy Ghost hath moved upon those waters, so, in Baptisme, let us not doubt of his power and effect upon all those children that dye so. We know no meanes how those waters could have produced a Menow, a Shrimp, without the Spirit of God had moved upon them; and by this motion of the Spirit of God, we know they produce Whales, and Leviathans. We know no ordinary meanes of any saving grace for a child, but Baptisme; neither are we to doubt of the fulnesse of salvation, in them that have received it. And for our selves, *Mergimur, et emergimus*, In Baptisme we are sunk under water, and then raised above the water againe; which was the manner of baptizing in the Christian Church, by immersion, and not by aspersion, till of late times: *Affectus, et amores*, sayes he, our corrupt affections, and our inordinate love of this world is that, that is to be drowned in us; *Amor securitatis*, A love of peace, and holy assurance, and acquiescence in God's Ordinance, is that that lifts us above water.

Therefore that Father puts all upon the due consideration of our Baptisme: And as St Hierome sayes, Certainly he that thinks upon the last Judgement advisedly, cannot sin then, So he that sayes with St Augustine, *Procede in confessione, fides mea*, Let me make every day to God, this confession, *Domine Deus meus, Sancte, Sancte, Sancte Domine Deus meus*, O Lord my God, O Holy, Holy, Holy Lord my God; *In nomine tuo Baptizatus sum*, I consider that I was baptized in thy name, and what thou promisedst me, and what I promised thee then, and can I sin this sin? can this sin stand with those conditions, those stipulations which passed between us then? The Spirit of God is motion, the Spirit of God is rest too; And in the due consideration of Baptisme, a true Christian is moved, and setled too; moved to a sense of the breach of his conditions, setled in the sense of the Mercy of his God, in the Merits of his Christ, upon his godly sorrow. So these waters are the waters of Baptisme.

Sin also is called by that name in the Scriptures, Water. The great whore sitteth upon many waters; she sits upon them, as upon Egges, and hatches Cockatrices, venomous and stinging sins; and yet pleasing, though venomous; which is the worst of sin, that it destroyes, and yet delights; for though they be called waters, yet that is said also, That the inhabitants of the earth were made drunk with the wine. Sin is wine at first, so farre as to allure, to intoxicate: It is water at last, so farre as to suffocate, to strangle. Christ Jesus way is to change water into wine; sorrow into joy: The Devil's way is to change wine into water; pleasure, and but false pleasure neither, into true bitternesse. The watrish wine, which is spoken of there, and called fornication, is idolatry, and the like. And in such a respect, God sayes to his people, What hast thou to doe in the way of Egypt? In the way of Egypt we cannot chuse but have something to doe; some conversation with men of an Idolatrous religion, we must needs have. But yet, What hast thou to doe in the way of Egypt, to drinke of the waters of Sihor? Or what hast thou to doe in the wayes of Assyria, to drink the waters of the River? Though we be bound to a peaceable conversation with men of an Idolatrous perswasion we are not bound to take in, to drink, to taste their errours. For this facility, and this indifferency to accompany men of divers religions, in the acts of their religion, this multiplicity will end in a nullity, and we shall hew to our selves Cisternes, broken Cisternes, that can hold no water; We shall scatter one religion into many, and those many shall vanish into none. Praise we God therefore, that the Spirit of God hath so moved upon these waters; these sinfull waters of superstition and idolatry, wherein our fore-Fathers were overwhelmed; that they have not swelled over us; For, then the cold North-winde blowes, and the water is congealed into Ice; Affliction overtakes us, damps us, stupifies us, and we finde no Religion to comfort us.

Affliction is as often expressed in this word, Waters, as sin. When thou passest through waters I will be with thee, and through the rivers, they shall not overflow thee. But then, the Spirit of God moves upon these waters too; and grace against sin, and deliverance from affliction, is as often expressed in waters, as either. Where God takes another Metaphore for judgement, yet he continues that of water for his mercy; In the fire of my jealousie have I spoken against them, (speaking of enemies; but then speaking of Israel) I will sprinkle cleane water upon you, and you shall be cleane. This is his way, and this is his measure;

He sprinkles enough at first to make us cleane; even the sprinkling of Baptisme cleanses us from orginall sin; but then he sets open the windowes of heaven, and he inlarges his Floodgates, I will poure out water upon the thirsty, and floods upon the dry ground: To them that thirst after him, he gives grace for grace; that is, present grace for an earnest of future grace; of subsequent grace, and concomitant grace, and auxiliant grace, and effectuall grace; grace in more formes, more notions, and in more operations, then the Schoole it selfe can tell how to name.

Thus the Spirit of God moves upon our waters. By faith Peter walked upon the waters; so we prevent occasions of tentation to sin, and sinke not in them, but walke above them. By godly exercises we swim through waters; so the Centurion commanded that they that could swim, should cast themselves into the sea; Men exercised in holinesse, can meet a tentation, or tribulation in the face, and not be shaked with it; weaker men, men that cannot swim, must be more wary of exposing themselves to dangers of tentation; A Court does some man no harme, when another finds tentation in a Hermitage. By repentance we saile through waters; by the assistance of God's ordinances in his Church, (which Church is the Arke) we attaine the harbour, peace of conscience, after a sin; But this Arke, this helpe of the Church we must have. God can save from dangers, though a man went to Sea without art, *Sine rate*, saies the Vulgat, without a Ship. But God hath given man *Prudentiam navifactivam*, saies our Holkot upon that place, and he would have that wisdome exercised. God can save without Preaching, and Absolution, and Sacraments, but he would not have his Ordinance neglected.

To end all with the end of all, Death comes to us in the name, and notion of waters, too, in the Scriptures. The Widow of Tekoah said to David in the behalfe of Absalon, by the Counsaile of Ioab, 'The water of death overflowes all; We must needs dye, saies she, and are as water spilt upon the ground, which cannot be gathered up againe: yet God devises meanes, that his banished, be not expelled from him.' So the Spirit of God moves upon the face of these waters, the Spirit of life upon the danger of death.

Consider the love, more than love, the study, more than study, the diligence of God, he devises meanes, that his banished, those whom sins, or death had banished, be not expelled from him. I sinned upon the strength of my youth, and God devised a meanes to reclaime me, an enfeebling sicknesse. I relapsed after my recovery, and God devised a meanes, an irrecoverable, a helpless Consumption to reclaime me; That affliction grew heavy upon me, and weighed me down even to a diffidence in God's mercy, and God devised a meanes, the comfort of the Angel of his Church, his Minister, The comfort of the Angel of the great Counsell, the body and blood of his Son Christ Jesus, at my transmigration. Yet he lets his correction proceed to death; I doe dye of that sicknesse, and God devises a meanes, that I, though banished, banished into the grave, shall not be expelled from him, a glorious Resurrection. We must needs dye and be as water spilt upon the ground, but yet God devises meanes, that his banished shall not be expelled from him.

And this is the motion, and this is the Rest of the Spirit of God upon those waters in this spirituall sense of these words, He brings us to a desire of Baptisme, he settles us in the sense of the obligation first, and then of the benefits of Baptisme. He suffers us to goe into the way of tentations, (for *Coluber in via*, and every calling hath particular tentations) and then he settles us, by his preventing, or his subsequent grace. He moves, in submitting us to tribulation, he settles us in finding, that our tribulations do best of all conforme us to his Son Christ Jesus. He moves in removing us by the hand of Death, and he settles us in an assurance, That it is he that now lets his Servants depart in peace; And he, who as he doth presently lay our soules in that safe Cabinet, the Bosome of Abraham, so he keeps an eye upon every graine, and atome of our dust, whither soever it be blowne, and keepes a roome at his owne right hand for that body, when that shall be re-united in a blessed Resurrection; And so 'The Spirit of God moved upon the face of the waters.'

The Call

Come, my Way, my Truth, my Life:
Such a Way as gives us breath;
Such a Truth as ends all strife;
Such as Life as killeth death.

Come, my Light, my Feast, my Strength:
Such a Light as shows a Feast;
Such a Feast that mends in length;
Such a Strength as makes his guest.

Come, my Joy, my Love my Heart:
Such a Joy as none can move;
Such a Love as none can part;
Such a Heart as joys in love.

George Herbert (1593–1633)

SERMON NINE

Jeremy Taylor

Jeremy Taylor (1613–1667) made a great splash with Holy Living *(1650) and an even greater one with* Holy Dying *in the following year. They remained popular books of devotion and even more widely bought gift books until well into the twentieth century. Taylor wrote these after the defeat of the royalist forces in the English Civil Wars of the 1640s. He had been chaplain to William Laud, the Archbishop of Canterbury who was executed in 1645. During the rule of Oliver Cromwell, Taylor lay low in Wales, building up a store of his remarkable sermons. When Charles II came in again in 1660, Taylor was immediately made Bishop of Down and Connor, in the north of Ireland. The diocese was dominated by Presbyterians, who, though of a royalist disposition, differed fundamentally from Taylor in their churchmanship. Almost all the rest of the population were Catholics, whom Taylor blamed for not speaking English but Irish.*

In his sermons, Taylor was not afraid of showing his learning. Though his nineteenth-century biographer A. F. Pollard wrote of the 'appalling length of his periods', Taylor's sermons sound easier than they look in print; all is clear when they are read aloud. The example here incorporated many quoted terms in Greek, which are immediately rendered in English, so I have dropped them; indeed the second half of the sermon considers marriage in Homer. This praise of marriage, of which we have here the first half, sat well with an Anglican view of the Church in society. As a composition it must have dazzled the discriminating audience of his time like a firework display.

The marriage ring; or,
The mysteriousness and duties of marriage

This is a great mystery, but I speak concerning Christ and the church. Nevertheless, let every one of you in particular so love his wife even as himself, and the wife see that she reverence her husband. (Ephesians 5:32)

The first blessing God gave to man was society, and that society was a marriage, and that marriage was confederate by God himself, and hallowed by a blessing: and at the same time, and for very many descending ages, not only by the instinct of nature, but by a super-added forwardness, God himself inspiring the desire, the world was most desirous of children, impatient of barrenness, accounting single life a curse, and a childless person hated by God. The world was rich and empty, and able to provide for a more numerous posterity than it had.

You that are rich, Numenius, you may multiply your family; poor men are not so fond of children, but when a family could drive their herds, and set their children upon camels, and lead them till they saw a fat soil watered with rivers, and there sit down without paying rent, they thought of nothing but to have great families, that their own relations might swell up to a patriarchate, and their children be enough to possess all the regions that they saw, and their grandchildren become princes, and themselves build cities and call them by the name of a child, and become the fountain of a nation. This was the consequent of the first blessing, 'increase and multiply'.

The next blessing was the promise of the Messias, and that also increased in men and women a wonderful desire of marriage: for as soon as God had chosen the family of Abraham to be the blessed line from whence the world's Redeemer should descend according to the flesh, every of his daughters hoped to have the honour to be His mother or His grandmother or something of His kindred: and to be childless in Israel was a sorrow to the Hebrew women great as the slavery of Egypt or their dishonours in the land of their captivity.

But when the Messias was come, and the doctrine was published, and His ministers but few, and His disciples were to suffer persecution and to be of an unsettled dwelling, and the nation of the Jews, in the bosom and society of which the Church especially did dwell, were to be scattered and broken all in pieces with fierce calamities, and the world was apt to calumniate and to suspect and dishonour Christians upon pretences and unreasonable jealousies,

81

and that to all these purposes the state of marriage brought many inconveniences; it pleased God in this new creation to inspire into the hearts of His servants a disposition and strong desires to live a single life, lest the state of marriage should in that conjunction of things become an accidental impediment to the dissemination of the gospel, which called men from a confinement in their domestic charges to travel, and flight, and poverty, and difficulty, and martyrdom: upon this necessity the apostles and apostolical men published doctrines declaring the advantages of single life, not by any commandment of the Lord, but by the spirit of prudence, 'for the present and then incumbent necessities', and in order to the advantages which did accrue to the public ministries and private piety. 'There are some', said our blessed Lord, 'who make themselves eunuchs for the kingdom of heaven', that is, for the advantages and the ministry of the gospel; *non ad vitae bonae meritum* as St Austin in the like case; not that it is a better service of God in itself, but that it is useful to the first circumstances of the gospel and the infancy of the kingdom, because the unmarried person 'is apt to spiritual and ecclesiastical employments': holy in his own person, and then sanctified to public ministries; and it was also of ease to the Christians themselves, because as then it was, when they were to flee, and to flee for aught they knew in winter, and they were persecuted to the four winds of heaven, and the nurses and the women with child were to suffer a heavier load of sorrow because of the imminent persecutions, and above all because of the great fatality of ruin upon the whole nation of the Jews, well it might be said by St Paul, 'such shall have trouble in the flesh', that is, they that are married shall, and so at that time they had: and therefore it was an act of charity to the Christians to give that counsel, 'I do this to spare you': for when the case was altered, and that storm was over, and the first necessities of the gospel served, and 'the sound was gone out into all nations'; in very many persons it was wholly changed, and not the married but the unmarried had 'trouble in the flesh'; and the state of marriage returned to its first blessing, 'and it was not good for man to be alone'.

But in this first interval, the public necessity and the private zeal mingling together did sometimes overact their love of single life, even to disparagement of marriage, and to the scandal of religion: which was increased by the occasion of some pious persons renouncing their contract of marriage, not consummate, with unbelievers. For when Flavia Domitilla being converted by Nereus and Achilleus the eunuchs refused to marry Aurelianus to whom she was contracted, if there were not some little envy and too sharp hostility in the eunuchs to a married state, yet Aurelianus thought himself an injured person, and caused St Clemens, who veiled her, and his spouse both, to die in the quarrel. St Thecla being converted by St Paul grew so in love with virginity, that she leaped back from the marriage of Tamyria where she was lately engaged. St Iphigenia denied to marry king Hyrtacus, and it is said to be done by the advice of St Matthew. And Susanna the niece of Dioclesian refused the love of Maximianus the emperor; and these all had been betrothed; and so did St Agnes, and St Felicula, and divers others then and afterwards: insomuch that it was reported among the gentiles, that the Christians did not only hate all that were not of their persuasion, but were enemies of the chaste laws of marriage; and indeed some that were called Christians were so, 'forbidding to marry, and commanding to abstain from meats'. Upon this occasion it grew necessary for the apostle to state the question right, and to do honour to the holy rite of marriage, and to snatch the mystery from the hands of zeal and folly, and to place it in Christ's right hand, that all its beauties might appear, and a present convenience might not bring in a false doctrine and a perpetual sin and an intolerable mischief. The apostle therefore, who himself had been a married man, but was now a widower, does explicate the mysteriousness of it, and describes its honours, and adorns it with rules and provisions of religion, that as it begins with honour, so it may proceed with piety and end with glory.

For although single life hath in it privacy and simplicity of affairs, such solitariness and sorrow, such leisure and unactive circumstances of living, that there are more spaces for religion if men would use them to these purposes; and because it may have in it much religion and prayers, and must have in it a perfect mortification of our strongest appetites, it is therefore a state of great excellency; yet concerning the state of marriage we are taught from scripture and the sayings of wise men great things and honourable. 'Marriage is honourable in all men'; so is not single life; for in some it is a snare and 'a trouble in the flesh', a prison of unruly desires which is attempted daily to be broken. Celibate or single life is never commanded, but in some cases marriage is, and he that burns sins often if he marries not; he that cannot contain must marry, and he that can contain is not tied to a single life, but may marry and not sin.

Marriage was ordained by God, instituted in paradise, was the relief of a natural necessity and the first blessing from the Lord; He gave to man not a friend, but a wife, that is, a friend and a wife too; for a good woman is in her soul the same that a man is, and she is a woman only in her body; that she may have the excellency of the one, and the usefulness of the other, and become amiable in both. It is the seminary of the Church, and daily brings forth sons and daughters unto God; it was ministered to by angels, and Raphael waited upon a young man that he might have a blessed marriage, and that that marriage might repair two sad families, and bless all their relatives. Our blessed Lord though He was born of a maiden, yet she was veiled under the cover of marriage, and she was married to a widower: for Joseph the supposed father of our Lord had children by a former wife.

The first miracle that ever Jesus did was to do honour to a wedding. Marriage was in the world before sin, and is in all ages of the world the greatest and most effective antidote against sin, in which all the world had perished if God had not made a remedy: and although sin hath soured marriage, and stuck the man's head with cares, and the woman's bed with sorrows in the production of children; yet these are but throes of life and glory, and 'she shall be saved in child-bearing, if she be found in faith and righteousness'. Marriage is a school and exercise of virtue; and though marriage hath cares, yet the single life hath desires which are more troublesome and more dangerous, and often end in sin, while the cares are but instances of duty and exercises of piety; and therefore if single life hath more privacy of devotion, yet marriage hath more neccessities and more variety of it, and is an exercise of more graces.

In two virtues celibate or single life may have the advantage of degrees ordinarily and commonly, that is, in chastity and devotion; but as in some persons this may fail, and it does in very many, and a married man may spend as much time in devotion as any virgins or widows do; yet as in marriage even those virtues of chastity and devotion are exercised, so in other instances this state hath proper exercises and trials for those graces for which single life can never be crowned. Here is the proper scene of piety and patience, of the duty of parents and the charity of relatives; here kindness is spread abroad, and love is united and made firm as a centre: marriage is the nursery of heaven; the virgin sends prayers to God, but she carries but one soul to Him; but the state of marriage fills up the numbers of the elect, and hath in it the labour of love, and the delicacies of friendship, the blessing of society, and the union of hands and hearts; it hath in it less of beauty, but more of safety, than the single life; it hath more care, but less danger; it is more merry, and more sad; is fuller of sorrows, and fuller of joys; it lies under more burdens, but it is supported by all the strengths of love and charity, and those burdens are delightful. Marriage is the mother of the world, and preserves kingdoms, and fills cities, and churches, and heaven itself.

Celibate, like the fly in the heart of an apple, dwells in a perpetual sweetness, but sits alone, and is confined and dies in singularity; but marriage, like the useful bee, builds a house and gathers sweetness from every flower, and labours and unites into societies and republics, and sends out colonies, and feeds the world with delicacies, and obeys their king, and keeps order, and exercises many virtues, and promotes the interest of mankind, and is that state of good things to which God hath designed the present constitution of the world.

Single life makes men in one instance to be like angels, but marriage in very many things makes the chaste pair to be like to Christ. 'This is a great mystery', but it is the symbolical and sacramental representment of the greatest mysteries of our religion.

Christ descended from His Father's bosom, and contracted His divinity with flesh and blood, and married our nature, and we became a Church, the spouse of the Bridegroom, which He cleansed with His blood, and gave her His Holy Spirit for a dowry, and heaven for a jointure, begetting children unto God by the gospel. This spouse He hath joined to Himself by an excellent charity, He feeds her at His own table, and lodges her nigh His own heart, provides for all her necessities, relieves her sorrows, determines her doubts, guides her wanderings; He is become her head, and she as a signet upon His right hand; He first indeed was betrothed to the synagogue and had many children by her, but she forsook His love, and then He married the church of the gentiles, and by her as by a second ventor had a more numerous issue; 'all the children dwell in the same house', and are heirs of the same promises, entitled to the same inheritance. Here is the eternal conjunction, the indissoluble knot, the exceeding love of Christ, the obedience of the spouse, the communicating of goods, the uniting of interests, the fruit of marriage, a celestial generation, a new creature: 'this is the sacramental mystery' represented by the holy rite of marriage; so that marriage is divine in its institution, sacred in its union, holy in the mystery, sacramental in its signification, honourable in its appellative, religious in its employments; it is advantage to the societies of men, and it is 'holiness to the Lord'.

Prayer

Almighty God, give us grace that we may cast away the works of darkness, and put upon us the armour of light, now in the time of this mortal life, in which thy Son Jesus Christ came to visit us in great humility; that in the last day, when he shall come again in his glorious majesty to judge both the quick and the dead, we may rise to the life immortal, through him that liveth and reigneth with thee and the Holy Ghost, now and ever. Amen

Book of Common Prayer, Collect of the First Sunday in Advent

SERMON TEN

John Bunyan

The great work of John Bunyan (1628–1688), Pilgrim's Progress, *had by the nineteenth century so established itself as a universally praised standard of English literature that its author's distinctively Nonconformist theology was almost overlooked. Bunyan, a tinker's son who fought in the army of the parliamentarians against the royalists in the Civil Wars, was imprisoned in 1660 in Bedford county jail for twelve years – not for his political loyalties but for preaching without a licence. In prison he wrote much, including the compelling work of autobiography* Grace Abounding to the Chief of Sinners. *During a later prison term he wrote* Pilgrim's Progress *(1678).*

Bunyan wrote a great deal, but it is not easy to classify some of his writing. Works such as Come and Welcome to Jesus Christ *follow the methodology of a sermon, but at much greater length than could be delivered at a sitting. The sermon here, reputed to be his last, contains characteristic Calvinist teaching on election and more warming words on being children of God.*

Mr Bunyan's last sermon, preached 19 August 1688

Which were born, not of blood, nor of the will of the flesh, nor of the will of man, but of God. (John 1:13)

The words have a dependence on what goes before, and therefore I must direct you to them for the right understanding of it. You have it thus: 'He came unto his own, and his own received him not; but as many as received him, to them gave he power to become the sons of God, even to them that believe on his name: which were born, not of blood, nor of the will of the flesh but of God.'

In the words before, you have two things. First, some of his own rejecting him, when he offered himself to them. Second, others of his own receiving him, and making him welcome; those that reject him, he also passes by; but those that receive him, he gives them power to become the sons of God.

Now, lest any one should look upon it as good luck or fortune, says he, they 'were born, not of blood, nor of the will of the flesh, nor of the will of man, but of God'. They that did not receive him, they were only born of flesh and blood; but those that receive him, they have God to their Father; they receive the doctrine of Christ with a vehement desire.

⋆   ⋆   ⋆

To explain the text:

First, I will show you what he means by blood. They that believe are born to it, as an heir is to an inheritance – they are born of God; not of flesh, nor of the will of man, but of God; not of blood, that is, not by generation, not born to the kingdom of heaven by the flesh, not because I am the son of a godly man or woman – that is meant by blood. He 'hath made of one blood all nations'. But when he says here, 'not of blood', he rejects all carnal privileges they did boast of: they boasted they were Abraham's seed; no, no, says he, it is not of blood; think not to say you have Abraham to your father; you must be born of God, if you go to the kingdom of heaven.

Second, 'Nor of the will of the flesh.' What must we understand by that? It is taken for those vehement inclinations that are in man, to all manner of looseness, fulfilling the desires of the flesh: that must not be understood here; men are not made the children of God by fulfilling their lustful desires. It must be understood here in the best sense: there is not only in carnal men a will to be vile, but there is in them a will to be saved also; a will to go to heaven also. But this it will not do; it will not privilege a man in the things of the kingdom of God: natural desires after the things of another world, they are not an argument to prove a man shall go to heaven whenever he dies. I am not a free-willer, I do abhor it; yet there is not the wickedest man but he desires, some time or other, to be saved; he will read some time or other, or, it may be, pray, but this will not do: 'It is not of him that willeth, nor of him that runneth, but of God that sheweth mercy.' There is willing and running and yet to no purpose (Romans, chapter 9, verse 16). Israel, which followed after the law of righteousness, have not obtained it. Here, I do not understand, as if the apostle had denied a virtuous course of life to be the way to heaven; but that a man without grace, though he have natural gifts, yet he shall not obtain privilege to go to heaven, and he the son of God. Though a man without grace may have a will to be saved, yet he cannot have that will God's way. Nature, it cannot know anything but the things of nature – the things of God knows no man but by the Spirit of God; unless the Spirit of God be in you, it will leave you on this side the gates of heaven. 'Not of blood, nor of the will of the flesh, nor of the will of man, but of God.' It may be, some may have a will, a desire that Ishmael may be saved; know this, it will not save thy child. If it was our will, I would have you all go to heaven. How many are there in the world that pray for their children, and cry for them, and are ready to die for them? and this will not do. God's will is the rule of all; it is only through Jesus Christ: 'which were born, not of flesh, nor of the will of man, but of God'.

★   ★   ★

Now I come to the doctrine.

Men that believe in Jesus Christ, to the effectual receiving of Jesus Christ, they are born to it. He does not say they *shall* be born to it, but they *are* born to it – born of God unto God and the things of God, before he receives God to eternal salvation. 'Except a man be born again, he cannot see the kingdom of God.' Now, unless he be born of God, he cannot see it: suppose the kingdom of God be what it will, he cannot see it before he be begotten of God. Suppose it be the gospel, he cannot see it before he be brought into a state of regeneration. Believing is the consequence of the new birth; 'not of blood, nor of the will of man, but of God'.

First, I will give you a clear description of it under one similitude or two. A child, before it be born into the world, is in the dark dungeon of its mother's womb: so a child of God, before he be born again, is the dark dungeon of sin, sees nothing of the kingdom of God: therefore it is called a new birth: the same soul has love way one in its carnal condition, another way when it is born again.

Second, compared to a birth, resembling a child in his mother's womb, so it is compared to a man being raised out of the grave; and to be born again, is to be raised out of the grave of sin; 'Awake, thou that sleepest, and arise from the dead, and Christ shall give thee light.' To be raised from the grave of sin is to be begotten and born; there is a famous instance of Christ; He is 'the first begotten of the dead'; He is the first-born from the dead, unto which our regeneration alludeth; that is, if you be born again by seeking those things that are above, then there is a similitude betwixt Christ's resurrection and the new birth; which was born, which was restored out of this dark world, and translated out of the kingdom of this dark world, into the kingdom of his dear Son, and made us live a new life – this is to be born again: and he that is delivered from the mother's womb, it is by the help of the mother; so he that is born of God, it is by the Spirit of God. I must give you a few consequences of a new birth.

★   ★   ★

First of all, a child, you know, is incident to cry as soon as it comes into the world; for if there be no noise, they say it is dead. You that are born of God, and Christians, if you be not criers, there is no spiritual life in you – if you be born of God, you are crying ones; as soon as he has raised you out of the dark dungeon of sin, you cannot but cry to God, What must I do to be saved? As soon as ever God had touched the jailer, he cries out, 'Men and brethren, what must I do to be saved?' Oh! How many prayerless professors is there in London that never pray! Coffee-houses will not let you pray, trades will not let you pray, looking-glasses will not let you pray; but if you was born of God, you would.

Second, it is not only natural for a child to cry, but it must crave the breast; it cannot live without the breast – therefore Peter makes it the true trial of a new born babe: the new born babe desires the sincere milk of the Word, that he may grow thereby: if you be born of God, make it manifest by desiring the breast of God. Do you long for the milk of the promises? A man lives one way when he is in the world, another way when he is brought unto Jesus Christ. They shall suck and be satisfied (Isaiah, chapter 66, verse 11); if you be born again, there is no satisfaction till you get the milk of God's Word into your souls. To 'suck and be satisfied with the breasts of her consolation'.

Oh! what is a promise to a carnal man? A whorehouse, it may be, is more sweet to him; but if you be born again, you cannot live without the milk of God's Word. What is a woman's breast to a horse? But what is it to a child? there is its comfort night and day, there is its succour night and day. Oh how loath are they it should be taken from them: minding heavenly things, says a carnal man, is but vanity; but to a child of God, there is his comfort.

Third, a child that is newly born, if it have not other comforts to keep it warm than it had in its mother's womb, it dies; it must have something got for its succour: so Christ had swaddling clothes prepared for him; so those that are born again, they must have some promise of Christ to keep them alive; those that are in a carnal state, they warm themselves with other things; but those that are born again, they cannot live without some promise of Christ to keep them alive; as he did to the poor infant in Ezechiel, chapter 16, verse 8: 'I covered thee with embroidered gold': and when women are with child, what fine things will they prepare for their child! Oh, but what fine things has Christ prepared to wrap all in that are born again! Oh what wrappings of gold has Christ prepared for all that are born again! Woman will dress their children, that every one may see them how fine they are; so he in Ezekiel, chapter 16, verse 11: 'I decked thee also with ornaments, and I put bracelets upon thine hands, and a chain on thy neck; and I put a jewel on thy forehead, and earrings in thine ears, and a beautiful crown upon thine head.' And, says he in verse 13, 'Thou didst prosper into a kingdom.' This is to set out nothing in the world but the righteousness of Christ and the graces of the Spirit, without which a new born babe cannot live, unless they have the golden righteousness of Christ.

Fourth, a child, when it is in its mother's lap, the mother takes great delight to have that which will be for its comfort; so it is with God's children, they shall be kept on his knee; 'They shall suck and be satisfied with the breasts of her consolations'; 'As one whom his mother comforteth, so will I comfort you.' There is a similitude in these things that nobody knows of, but those that are born again.

Fifth, there is usually some similitude betwixt the father and the child. It may be the child looks like its father; so those that are born again, they have a new similitude – they have the image of Jesus Christ. Every one that is born of God has something of the features of heaven upon him. Men love those children that are likest them most usually; so does God his children, therefore they are called the children of God; but others do not look like him, therefore they are called Sodomites.

Christ describes children of the devil by their features – the children of the devil, his works they will do; all works of unrighteousness, they are the devil's works: if you are earthly, you have borne the image of the earthly; if heavenly, you have borne the image of the heavenly.

Sixth, when a man has a child, he trains him up to his own liking – they have learned the custom of their father's house; so are those that are born of God – they have learned the custom of the true church of God: there they learn to cry 'My Father' and 'My God'; they are brought up in God's house, they learn the method and form of God's house, for regulating their lives in this world.

Seventh, children, it is natural for them to depend upon their father for what they want; if they want a pair of shoes, they go and tell him; if they want bread, they go and tell him; so should the children of God do. Do you want spiritual bread? Go tell God of it. Do you want strength of grace? Ask it of God. Do you want strength against Satan's temptations? Go and tell God of it. When

the devil tempts you, run home and tell your heavenly Father –
go, pour out your complaints to God; this is natural to children; if
any wrong them, they go and tell their father; so do those that are
born of God, when they meet with temptations go and tell God of
them.

The application
The first use is this, To make a strict inquiry whether you be born
of God or not; examine by those things laid down before, of a child
of nature and a child of grace. Are you brought out of the dark
dungeon of this world into Christ? Have you learned to cry, 'My
Father?' (Jeremiah, chapter 3, verse 4): 'And I said, Thou shalt call
me, My Father.' All God's children are criers – cannot you be quiet
without you have a bellyful of the milk of God's Word? Cannot
you be satisfied without you have peace with God? Pray you,
consider it, and be serious with yourselves; if you have not these
marks, you will fall short of the kingdom of God – you shall never
have an interest there; 'there' is no intruding. They will say, 'Lord,
Lord, open to us'; and he will say, 'I know you not.' No child of
God, no heavenly inheritance. We sometimes give something to
those that are not our children, but we do not give them our lands.
Oh do not flatter yourselves with a portion among the sons, unless
you live like sons. When we see a king's son play with a beggar, this
is unbecoming; so if you be the king's children, live like the king's
children; if you be risen with Christ, set your affections on things
above, and not on things below; when you come together, talk of
what your Father promised you; you should all love your Father's
will, and be content and pleased with the exercises you meet with
in the world. If you are the children of God, live together lovingly;
if the world quarrel with you, it is no matter; but it is sad if you
quarrel together; if this be amongst you, it is a sign of ill-breeding; it
is not according to the rules you have in the Word of God. Dost
thou see a soul that has the image of God in him? Love him, love
him; say, This man and I must go to heaven one day; serve one
another, do good for one another; and if any wrong you, pray to
God to right you, and love the brotherhood.

Lastly, If you be the children of God, learn that lesson – Gird up the loins of your mind, as obedient children, not fashioning yourselves according to your former conversation; but be ye holy in all manner of conversation. Consider that the holy God is your Father, and let this oblige go you to live like the children of God, that you may look your Father in the face, with comfort, another day.

Help for prisoners:
Prayer after sentence of death

O God, thy will be done. The Lord has given, the Lord has taken away, blessed be the name of the Lord. I received my life from thy hands, and ought not I to surrender it when thou demandest it of me? Now thou hast sent me a summons, and in this manifested thy will for me; and as I acknowledge thee to be my Lord, so I know it is my duty to obey; I wish I could do it cheerfully and without reluctance; but though nature be unwilling, yet, notwithstanding all unwillingness, behold I now bow down, and with all possible submission pronounce from heart, Lord thy will be done on earth as it is in heaven. Lord, thy will be done on earth as it is in heaven. Lord, thy will be done on earth as it is in heaven.

John Gother (died 1704)

SERMON ELEVEN

❧

Jonathan Swift

Swift's Gulliver's Travels *has been regarded as a children's book only because it narrates a fantastic voyage. Like most of his work it was a satire. His satiric skill, fired by* saeva indignatio *(fierce indignation), as his epitaph puts it, is perhaps most violent in* A Modest Proposal, *advocating the eating of Irish babies. Swift (1667–1745) was ordained in 1695 but hardly seems a clergyman from most of his writings, which appeared anonymously. Some of his poetry is, not pornographic, but obscene in the way it treats of a deep sexual disgust. Yet Swift, in his letters, showed a profound self-knowledge.*

He was made the (Anglican) Dean of St Patrick's Cathedral, Dublin in 1714, but did not care to publish sermons beyond the handful that include this composition, which drily displays his knowledge of ridicule and of the weaknesses of men.

Upon sleeping in church

And there sat in a window a certain young man, named Eutychus, being fallen into a deep sleep; and as Paul was long preaching, he sunk down with sleep, and fell down from the third loft, and was taken up dead. (Acts 20:9)

I have chosen these words with design, if possible, to disturb some part in this audience of half an hour's sleep, for the convenience and exercise whereof this place, at this season of the day, is very much celebrated.

There is indeed one mortal disadvantage to which all preaching is subject; that those who, by the wickedness of their lives, stand in greatest need, have usually the smallest share; for either they are absent upon the account of idleness, or spleen, or hatred to religion, or in order to doze away the intemperance of the week; or, if they do come, they are sure to employ their minds rather any other way, than regarding or attending to the business of the place.

The accident which happened to this young man in the text, hath not been sufficient to discourage his successors: But because the preachers now in the world, however they may exceed St Paul in the art of setting men to sleep, do extremely fall short of him in the working of miracles; therefore men are become so cautious as to choose more safe and convenient stations and postures for taking their repose, without hazard of their persons; and, upon the whole matter, choose rather to trust their destruction to a miracle, than their safety. However, this being not the only way by which the lukewarm Christians and scorners of the age discover their neglect and contempt of preaching, I shall enter expressly into consideration of this matter, and order my discourse in the following method:

First: I shall produce several instances to shew the great neglect of preaching now amongst us.

Second: I shall reckon up some of the usual quarrels men have against preaching.

Third: I shall set forth the great evil of this neglect and contempt of preaching, and discover the real causes from whence it proceedeth.

Lastly: I shall offer some remedies against this great and spreading evil.

★   ★   ★

First, I shall produce certain instances to shew the great neglect of preaching now among us.

These may be reduced under two heads. First, men's absence from the service of the Church; and secondly, their misbehaviour when they are here.

The first instance of men's neglect, is in their frequent absence from the church. There is no excuse so trivial that will not pass upon some men's consciences to excuse their attendance at the public worship of God. Some are so unfortunate as to be always indisposed on the Lord's day, and think nothing so unwholesome as the air of a church. Others have their affairs so oddly contrived, as to be always unluckily prevented by business. With some it is a great mark of wit, and deep understanding, to stay at home on Sundays. Others again discover strange fits of laziness, that seize them, particularly on that day, and confine them to their beds. Others are absent out of mere contempt of religion, And, lastly, there are not a few who look upon it as a day of rest, and therefore claim the privilege of their cattle, to keep the Sabbath by eating, drinking, and sleeping, after the toil and labour of the week. Now in all this the worst circumstance is that these persons are such whose companies are most required, and who stand most in need of a physician.

Secondly: Men's great neglect and contempt of preaching, appear by their misbehaviour when at church. If the audience were to be ranked under several heads, according to their behaviour, when the word of God is delivered, how small a number would appear of those who receive it as they ought? How much of the seed then sown would be found to fall by the way-side, upon stony ground or among thorns? And how little good ground would there be to take it? A preacher cannot look round from the pulpit without observing that some are in a perpetual whisper, and, by their air and gesture, give occasion to suspect, that they are in those very minutes defaming their neighbour. Others have their eyes and imagination constantly engaged in such a circle of objects, perhaps to gratify the most unwarrantable desires, that they never once attend to the business of the place; the sound of the preacher's words doth not so much as once interrupt them. Some have their minds wandering among idle, worldly, or vicious thoughts. Some lie at catch to ridicule whatever they hear, and with much wit and humour provide a stock of laughter, by furnishing themselves from the pulpit.

But, of all misbehaviour, none is comparable to that of those who come here to sleep; opium is not so stupefying to many persons as an afternoon sermon. Perpetual custom hath so brought it about, that the words, of whatever preacher, become only a sort of uniform sound at a distance, than which nothing is more effectual to lull the senses. For, that it is the very sound of the sermon which bindeth up their faculties, is manifest from hence, because they all awake so very regularly as soon as it ceaseth, and with much devotion receive the blessing, dozed and besotted with indecencies I am ashamed to repeat.

★   ★   ★

I proceed secondly to reckon up some of the usual quarrels men have against preaching, and to shew the unreasonableness of them.

Such unwarrantable demeanour as I have described, among Christians, in the house of God, in a solemn assembly, while their faith and duty are explained and delivered, have put those who are guilty upon inventing some excuses to extenuate their fault. This they do by turning the blame either upon the particular preacher, or upon preaching in general.

First, they object against the particular preacher; his manner, his delivery, his voice are disagreeable, his style and expression are flat and low; some improper and absurd; the matter is heavy, trivial and insipid; sometimes despicable, and perfectly ridiculous; or else, on the other side, he runs up into unintelligible speculation, empty notions, and abstracted flights, all clad in words above usual understandings.

Secondly, they object against preaching in general; it is a perfect road of talk; they know already whatever can be said; they have heard the same an hundred times over. They quarrel that preachers do not relieve an old beaten subject with wit and invention; and that now the art is lost of moving men's passions, so common among the ancient orators of Greece and Rome. These, and the like objections are frequently in the mouths of men who despise the 'foolishness of preaching'. But let us examine the reasonableness of them.

The doctrine delivered by all preachers is the same: 'So we preach, and so ye believe.' But the manner of delivering is suited to the skill and abilities of each, which differ in preachers just as in the rest of mankind. However, in personal dislikes of a particular preacher, are these men sure they are always in the right? Do they consider how mixed a thing is every audience, whose taste and judgement differ, perhaps, every day, not only from each other, but themselves? And how to calculate a discourse, that shall exactly suit them all, is beyond the force and reach of human reason, knowledge, or invention. Wit and eloquence are shining qualities, that God hath imparted in great degrees to very few, nor any more to be expected, in the generality of any rank among men, than riches and honour.

But further: If preaching in general be all old and beaten, and that they are already so well acquainted with it, more shame and guilt to them who so little edify by it. But these men, whose ears are so delicate as not to endure a plain discourse of religion, who expect a constant supply of wit and eloquence on a subject handled 'so many thousand times'; what will they say when we turn the objection upon themselves, who, with all the rude and profane liberty of discourse they take, upon so many thousand subjects, are so dull as to furnish nothing but tedious repetitions, and little paltry, nauseous common-places, so vulgar, so worn, or so obvious, as, upon any other occasion, but that of advancing vice, would be hooted off the stage?

Nor, lastly, are preachers justly blamed for neglecting human oratory to move the passions, which is not the business of a Christian orator, whose office it is only to work upon faith and reason. All other eloquence hath been a perfect cheat, to stir up men's passions against truth and justice, for the service of a faction, to put false colours upon things, and by an amusement of agreeable words, make the worse reason appear to be the better. This is certainly not to be allowed in Christian eloquence, and, therefore, St Paul took quite the other course; he 'came not with the excellency of words, or enticing speech of men's wisdom, but in plain evidence of the Spirit and power'. And perhaps it was for that reason the young man Eutychus, used to the Grecian eloquence, grew tired and fell so fast asleep.

*　　*　　*

I go on, thirdly, to set forth the great evil of this neglect and scorn of preaching, and to discover the real causes from whence it proceedeth. I think it is obvious, that this neglect of preaching hath very much occasioned the great decay of religion among us. To this may be imputed no small part of that contempt some men bestow on the clergy; for, whoever talketh without being regarded, is sure to be despised. To this we owe, in a great measure, the spreading of atheism and infidelity among us; for religion, like all other things, is soonest put out of countenance by being ridiculed. The scorn of preaching might perhaps have been at first introduced by men of nice ears and refined taste; but it is now become a spreading evil, through all degrees, and both sexes; for, since sleeping, talking, and laughing are qualities sufficient to furnish out a critic, the meanest and most ignorant have set up a title, and succeeded in it as well as their betters. Thus are the last efforts of reforming mankind rendered wholly useless: 'How shall they hear', saith the apostle, 'without a preacher?' But, if they have a preacher, and make it a point of wit or breeding not to hear him, what remedy is left?

To this neglect of preaching, we may also entirely impute that gross ignorance among us in the very principles of religion, which it is amazing to find in persons who very much value their own knowledge and understanding in other things; yet, it is a visible, inexcusable ignorance, even in the meanest among us, considering the many advantages they have of learning their duty. And it hath been the great encouragement to all manner of vice: For, in vain we preach down sin to a people, 'whose hearts are waxed gross, whose ears are dull of hearing, and whose eyes are closed'. Therefore Christ Himself, in His discourses, frequently rouseth up the attention of the multitude, and of His disciples themselves, with this expression, 'He that hath ears to hear, let him hear.'

But, among all neglects of preaching, none is so fatal as that of sleeping in the house of God; a scorner may listen to truth and reason, and in time grow serious; an unbeliever may feel the pangs of a guilty conscience; one whose thoughts or eyes wander among other objects, may, by a lucky word, be called back to attention: But the sleeper shuts up all avenues to his soul: He is 'like the deaf adder, that hearkeneth not to the voice of the charmer, charm he never so wisely'. And, we may preach with as good success to the grave that is under his feet.

But the great evil of this neglect will further yet appear, from considering the real causes whence it proceedeth; whereof the first, I take to be, an evil conscience. Many men come to church to save or gain a reputation; or because they will not be singular, but comply with an established custom; yet, all the while, they are loaded with the guilt of old rooted sins. These men can expect to hear of nothing but tenors and threatenings, their sins laid open in true colours, and eternal misery the reward of them; therefore, no wonder they stop their ears, and divert their thoughts, and seek any amusement rather than stir the hell within them.

Another cause of this neglect is, a heart set upon worldly things. Men whose minds are much enslaved to earthly affairs all the week cannot disengage or break the chain of their thoughts so suddenly as to apply to a discourse that is wholly foreign to what they have most at heart. Tell a usurer of charity, and mercy, and restitution, you talk to the deaf; his heart and soul, with all his senses, are got among his bags, or he is gravely asleep, and dreaming of a mortgage. Tell a man of business, that the cares of the world choke the good seed; that we must not encumber our-selves with much serving; that the salvation of his soul is the one thing necessary: You see, indeed, the shape of a man before you, but his faculties are all gone off among clients and papers, thinking how to defend a bad cause, or find flaws in a good one; or, he weareth out the time in drowsy nods.

A third cause of the great neglect and scorn of preaching, ariseth from the practice of men who set up to decry and disparage religion; these, being zealous to promote infidelity and vice, learn a rote of buffoonery that serveth all occasions, and refutes the strongest arguments for piety and good manners. These have a set of ridicule calculated for all sermons, and all preachers, and can be extreme witty as often as they please upon the same fund.

★   ★   ★

Let me now, in the last place, offer some remedies against this great evil. It will be one remedy against the contempt of preach-ing, rightly to consider the end for which it was designed. There are many who place abundance of merit in going to church, although it be with no other prospect but that of being well entertained, wherein if they happen to fail, they return wholly disappointed. Hence it is become an impertinent vein among people of all sorts to hunt after what they call a good sermon, as if it were a matter of pastime and diversion.

Our business, alas! is quite another thing, either to learn, or, at least, be reminded of our duty, to apply the doctrines delivered, compare the rules we hear with our lives and actions, and find wherein we have transgressed. These are the dispositions men should bring into the house of God, and then they will be little concerned about the preacher's wit or eloquence, nor be curious to enquire out his faults and infirmities, but consider how to correct their own.

Another remedy against the contempt of preaching, is, that men would consider, whether it be not reasonable to give more allowances for the different abilities of preachers than they usually do; refinements of style, and flights of wit, as they are not properly the business of any preacher, so they cannot possibly be the talents of all. In most other discourse, men are satisfied with sober sense and plain reason; and, as understandings usually go, even that is not over frequent. Then why they should be so over nice in expectation of eloquence, where it is neither necessary nor convenient, is hard to imagine.

Lastly: The scorners of preaching would do well to consider, that this talent of ridicule, they value so much, is a perfection very easily acquired, and applied to all things whatsoever; neither is anything at all the worse, because it is capable of being perverted to burlesque: Perhaps it may be the more perfect upon that score; since we know, the most celebrated pieces have been thus treated with greatest success. It is in any man's power to suppose a fool's cap on the wisest head, and then laugh at his own supposition. I think there are not many things cheaper than supposing and laughing; and if the uniting these two talents can bring a thing into contempt, it is hard to know where it may end.

To conclude: These considerations may, perhaps, have some effect while men are awake; but what arguments shall we use to the sleeper? What methods shall we take to hold open his eyes? Will he be moved by considerations of common civility? We know it is reckoned a point of very bad manners to sleep in private company, when, perhaps, the tedious impertinence of many talkers would render it at least as excusable as at the dullest sermon. Do they think it a small thing to watch four hours at a play, where all virtue and religion are openly reviled; and can they not watch one half hour to hear them defended? Is this to deal like a judge, (I mean like a good judge) to listen on one side of the cause, and sleep on the other?

I shall add but one word more: That this indecent sloth is very much owing to that luxury and excess men usually practise upon this day, by which half the service thereof is turned to sin; men dividing the time between God and their bellies, when after a gluttonous meal, their senses dozed and stupefied, they retire to God's house to sleep out the afternoon. Surely, brethren, these things ought not so to be.

'He that hath ears to hear, let him hear.' And God give us all grace to hear and receive His holy word to the salvation of our own souls.

Melancholy

O, thou which on the mountain's brow,
　　By night didst pray alone;
In the cold night didst pay thy vow,
And in humiliation bow,
　　To thrones and pow'rs thine own,

Tell us, for thou the best can tell,
　　What Melancholy means?
A guise in them that wear it well,
That goes to music to dispel
　　Dark thoughts and gloomier scenes.

Say, didst thou solitude desire
    Or wert thou driv'n away,
By rank desertion to retire,
Without or bed, or food, or fire,
    For all thy foes to pray.

Yet thou didst preach of future bliss,
    Peace permanent above,
Of truth and mercy's holy kiss,
Those joys that none that love thee miss,
    O give us grace to love.

Christopher Smart (1722–1771)
From *Hymns for the Amusement of Children*

SERMON TWELVE

Jonathan Edwards

The Great Awakening, as the Christian revival beginning in America in the 1730s became known, took Jonathan Edwards (1703–1758) as its exemplar. He was a Connecticut man, studied at Yale and in 1729 was appointed pastor at Northampton, Massachusetts. After a time his sermons provoked his congregation into self-examination and conversion. Edwards preached a strict Calvinism of predestination and election; some have seen as loathsome his portrayal of God as creator of men and women destined to damnation.

The spiritual awakening that Edwards set off was given a new impetus from the Methodist preaching of George Whitefield, who arrived in New England in 1740. Edwards himself was dismissed as Pastor of Northampton in 1750, after doctrinal disagreements. He became a missionary to American Indians, and had taken up the post of president of the College of New Jersey (later Princeton) in 1758 when he was killed by a smallpox inoculation.

The sermon here (1741) makes breathtaking use of vivid language and is tour de force *of Edwards's approach.*

Their foot shall slide in due time. (Deuteronomy 32:35)

In this verse is threatened the vengeance of God on the wicked unbelieving Israelites, who were God's visible people, and who lived under the means of grace; but who, notwithstanding all God's wonderful works towards them, remained void of counsel, having no understanding in them. Under all the cultivations of heaven, they brought forth bitter and poisonous fruit; as in the two verses next preceding the text.

The expression I have chosen for my text, 'Their foot shall slide in due time', seems to imply the following things, relating to the punishment and destruction to which these wicked Israelites were exposed:

First: that they were always exposed to *destruction*; as one that stands or walks in slippery places is always exposed to fall. This is implied in the manner of their destruction coming upon them, being represented by their foot sliding. The same is expressed (Psalm 73, verse 18): 'Surely thou didst set them in slippery places; thou castedst them down into destruction.'

Second: it implies, that they were always exposed to sudden unexpected destruction. As he that walks in slippery places is every moment liable to fall, he cannot foresee one moment whether he shall stand or fall the next; and when he does fall, he falls at once without warning: Which is also expressed in Psalm 73, verses 18, 19: 'Surely thou didst set them in slippery places; thou castedst them down into destruction: How are thy brought into desolation as in a moment!'

Third: another thing implied is, that they are liable to fall of *themselves*, without being thrown down by the hand of another; as he that stands or walks on slippery ground needs nothing but his own weight to throw him down.

Fourth: that the reason why they are not fallen already, and do not fall now, is only that God's appointed time is not come. For it is said, that when due time, or appointed time comes, *their foot shall slide*. Then they shall be left to fall, as they are inclined by their own weight. God will not hold them up in these slippery places any longer, but will let them go; and then, at that very instant, they shall fall into destruction; as he that stands on such slippery declining ground, on the edge of a pit, he cannot stand alone, when he is let go he immediately falls and is lost.

★　　　★　　　★

The observation from the words that I would insist upon is this: 'There is nothing that keeps wicked men at any one moment out of hell, but the mere pleasure of God': By the *mere* pleasure of God, I mean his *sovereign* pleasure, his arbitrary will, restrained by no obligation, hindered by no manner of difficulty, any more than if nothing else but God's mere will had in the least degree, or in any respect whatsoever, any hand in the preservation of wicked men one moment. The truth of this observation may appear by the following considerations.

111

First: there is no want of *power* in God to cast wicked men into hell at any moment. Men's hands cannot be strong when God rises up: The strongest have no power to resist him, nor can any deliver out of his hands. He is not only able to cast wicked men into hell, but he can most easily do it. Sometimes an earthly prince meets with a great deal of difficulty to subdue a rebel, who has found means to fortify himself, and has made himself strong by the numbers of his followers. But it is not so with God. There is no fortress that is any defence from the power of God. Though hand join in hand, and vast multitudes of God's enemies combine and associate themselves, they are easily broken in pieces. They are as great heaps of light chaff before the whirlwind; or large quantities of dry stubble before devouring flames. We find it easy to tread on and crush a worm that we see crawling on the earth; so it is easy for us to cut or singe a slender thread that any thing hangs by: thus easy is it for God, when he pleases, to cast his enemies down to hell. What are we, that we should think to stand before him, at whose rebuke the earth trembles, and before whom the rocks are thrown down?

Second: they *deserve* to be cast into hell; so that divine justice never stands in the way, it makes no objection against God's using his power at any moment to destroy them. Yea, on the contrary, justice calls aloud for an infinite punishment of their sins. Divine justice says of the tree that brings forth such grapes of Sodom, 'Cut it down, why cumbereth it the ground?' The sword of divine justice is every moment brandished over their heads. And it is nothing but the hand of arbitrary mercy, and God's mere will, that holds it back.

Third: they are already under a sentence of *condemnation* to hell. They do not only justly deserve to be cast down thither, but the sentence of the law of God, that eternal and immutable rule of righteousness that God has fixed between him and mankind, is gone out against them, and stands against them; so that they are bound over already to hell. 'He that believeth not is condemned already.' So that every unconverted man properly belongs to hell; that is his place; from thence he is: 'Ye are from beneath.' And thither he is bound; it is the place that justice and God's word, and the sentence of his unchangeable law, assign to him.

Fourth: they are now the objects of that very same *anger* and wrath of God, that is expressed in the torments of hell. And the reason why they do not go down to hell at each moment, is not because God, in whose power they are, is not then very angry with them; as he is with many miserable creatures now tormented in hell, who there feel and bear the fierceness of his wrath. Yea, God is a great deal more angry with great numbers that are now on earth; yea, doubtless, with many that are now in this congregation, who it may be are at ease, than he is with many of those who are now in the flames of hell.

So that it is not because God is unmindful of their wickedness, and does not resent it, that he does not let loose his hand and cut them off. God is not altogether such an one as themselves, though they may imagine him to be so. The wrath of God burns against them, their damnation does not slumber; the pit is prepared, the fire is made ready, the furnace is now hot, ready to receive them; the flames do now rage and glow. The glittering sword is whet, and held over them, and the pit hath opened its mouth under them.

Fifth: the *devil* stands ready to fall upon them, and seize them as his own, at what moment God shall permit him. They belong to him, he has their souls in his possession, and under his dominion. The scripture represents them as his goods. The devils watch them; they are ever by them, at their right hand; they stand waiting for them, like greedy hungry lions that see their prey, and expect to have it, but are for the present kept back. If God should withdraw his hand, by which they are restrained, they would in one moment fly upon their poor souls. The old serpent is gaping for them; hell opens its mouth wide to receive them; and if God should permit it, they would be hastily swallowed up and lost.

Sixth: there are in the souls of wicked men those hellish *principles* reigning, that would presently kindle and flame out into hell fire, if it were not for God's restraints. There is laid in the very nature of carnal men, a foundation for the torments of hell. There are those corrupt principles, in reigning power in them, and in full possession of them, that are seeds of hell fire. These principles are active and powerful, exceeding violent in their nature, and if it were not for the restraining hand of God upon them, they would soon break out, they would flame out after the same manner as the same corruptions, the same enmity does in the hearts of damned souls, and would beget the same torments as they do in them.

The souls of the wicked are in scripture compared to the troubled sea (Isaiah, chapter 13, verse 20). For the present, God restrains their wickedness by his mighty power, as he does the raging waves of the troubled sea, saying, 'Hitherto shalt thou come, but no further'; but if God should withdraw that restraining power, it would soon carry all before it. Sin is the ruin and misery of the soul; it is destructive in its nature; and if God should leave it without restraint, there would need nothing else to make the souls perfectly miserable. The corruption of the heart of man is immoderate and boundless in its fury; and while wicked men live here, it is like fire pent up by God's restraints, whereas if it were let loose, it would set on fire the course of nature; and as the heart is now a sink of sin, so, if sin was not restrained, it would immediately turn the soul into a fiery oven, or a furnace of fire and brimstone.

Seventh: it is no security to wicked men for one moment, that there are no visible means of death at hand. It is no security to a natural man, that he is now in health, and that he does not see which way he should now immediately go out of the world by any accident, and that there is no visible danger in any respect in his circumstances. The manifold and continual experience of the world in all ages, shews this is no evidence, that a man is not on the very brink of eternity, and that the next step will not be into another world. The unseen, unthought-of ways and means of persons going suddenly out of the world are innumerable and inconceivable.

Unconverted men walk over the pit of hell on a rotten

covering, and there are innumerable places in this covering so weak that they will not bear their weight, and these places are not seen. The arrows of death fly unseen at noon-day; the sharpest sight cannot discern them. God has so many different un-searchable ways of taking wicked men out of the world and sending them to hell, that there is nothing to make it appear, that God had need to be at the expence of a miracle, or go out of the ordinary course of his providence, to destroy any wicked man, at any moment. All the means that there are of sinners going out of the world, are so in God's hands, and so universally and absolutely subject to his power and determination, that it does not depend at all the less on the mere will of God, whether sinners shall at any moment go to hell, than if means were never made use of, or at all concerned in the case.

Eighth: natural men's prudence and care to preserve their own lives, or the care of others to preserve them, do not secure them a moment. To this, divine providence and universal experience do also bear testimony. There is this clear evidence that men's own wisdom is no security to them from death; that if it were other-wise we should see some difference between the wise and politic men of the world, and others, with regard to their liableness to early and unexpected death; but how is it in fact? 'How dieth the wise man? Even as the fool.'

Ninth: all wicked men's pains and *contrivance* which they use to escape hell, while they continue to reject Christ, and so remain wicked men, do not secure them from hell one moment. Almost every natural man that hears of hell, flatters himself that he shall escape it; he depends upon himself for his own security; he flatters himself in what he has done, in what he is now doing, or what he intends to do. Every one lays out matters in his own mind how he shall avoid damnation, and flatters himself that he contrives well for himself, and that his schemes will not fail. They hear indeed that there are but few saved, and that the greater part of men that have died heretofore are gone to hell; but each one imagines that he lays out matters better for his own escape than others have done. He does not intend to come to that place of torment; he says within himself, that he intends to take effectual care, and to order matters so for himself as not to fail.

But the foolish children of men miserably delude themselves in their own schemes, and in confidence in their own strength and wisdom; they trust to nothing but a shadow. The greater part of those who heretofore have lived under the same means of grace, and are now dead, are undoubtedly gone to hell; and it was not because they were not as wise as those who are now alive; it was not because they did not lay out matters as well for themselves to secure their own escape. If we could speak with them, and inquire of them, one by one, whether they expected, when alive, and when they used to hear about hell, ever to be the subjects of that misery; we, doubtless, should hear one and another reply, 'No, I never intended to come here: I had laid out matters otherwise in my mind; I thought I should contrive well for myself: I thought my scheme good. I intended to take effectual care; but it came upon me unexpected; I did not look for it at that time, and in that manner; it came as a thief; Death outwitted me: God's wrath was too quick for me. Oh, my cursed foolishness! I was flattering myself, and pleasing myself with vain dreams of what I would do hereafter; and when I was saying, Peace and safety, then sudden destruction came upon me.'

God has laid himself under *no obligation*, by any promise to keep any natural man out of hell one moment. God certainly has made no promises either of eternal life, or of any deliverance or preservation from eternal death, but what are contained in the covenant of grace, the promises that are given in Christ, in whom all the promises are yea and amen. But surely they have no interest in the promises of the covenant of grace who are not the children of the covenant, who do not believe in any of the promises, and have no interest in the Mediator of the covenant.

So that, whatever some have imagined and pretended about promises made to natural men's earnest seeking and knocking, it is plain and manifest, that whatever pains a natural man takes in religion, whatever prayers he makes, till he believes in Christ,

God is under no manner of obligation to keep him a moment from eternal destruction.

So that, thus it is that natural men are held in the hand of God, over the pit of hell; they have deserved the fiery pit, and are already sentenced to it; and God is dreadfully provoked, his anger is as great towards them as to those that are actually suffering the executions of the fierceness of his wrath in hell, and they have done nothing in the least to appease or abate that anger, neither is God in the least bound by any promise to hold them up one moment; the devil is waiting for them, hell is gaping for them, the flames gather and flash about them, and would fain lay hold on them, and swallow them up; the fire pent up in their own hearts is struggling to break out; and they have no interest in any Mediator, there are no means within reach that can be any security to them. In short, they have no refuge, nothing to take hold of; all that preserves them every moment is the mere arbitrary will, and uncovenanted, unobliged forbearance of an incensed God.

The use of this awful subject may be for awakening unconverted persons in this congregation. This that you have heard is the case of every one of you that are out of Christ. – That world of misery, that lake of burning brimstone, is extended abroad under you. There is the dreadful pit of the glowing flames of the wrath of God; there is hell's wide gaping mouth open; and you have nothing to stand upon, nor any thing to take hold of; there is nothing between you and hell but the air; it is only the power and mere pleasure of God that holds you up.

You probably are not sensible of this; you find you are kept out of hell, but do not see the hand of God in it; but look at other things, as the good state of your bodily constitution, your care of your own life, and the means you use for your own preservation. But indeed these things are nothing; if God should withdraw his hand, they would avail no more to keep you from falling, than the thin air to hold up a person that is suspended in it.

Your wickedness makes you as it were heavy as lead, and to tend downwards with great weight and pressure towards hell; and if God should let you go, you would immediately sink and swiftly descend and plunge into the bottomless gulf, and your healthy constitution, and your own care and prudence, and best contrivance, and all your righteousness, would have no more influence to uphold you and keep you out of hell, than a spider's web would have to stop a falling rock. Were it not for the sovereign pleasure of God, the earth would not bear you one moment; for you are a burden to it; the creation groans with you; the creature is made subject to the bondage of your corruption, not willingly; the sun does not willingly shine upon you to give you light to serve sin and Satan; the earth does not willingly yield her increase to satisfy your lusts; nor is it willingly a stage for your wickedness to be acted upon; the air does not willingly serve you for breath to maintain the flame of life in your vitals, while you spend your life in the service of God's enemies. God's creatures are good, and were made for men to serve God with, and do not willingly subserve to any other purpose, and groan when they are abused to purposes so directly contrary to their nature and end. And the world would spew you out, were it not for the sovereign hand of him who hath subjected it in hope. There are the black clouds of God's wrath now hanging directly over your heads, full of the dreadful storm, and big with thunder; and were it not for the restraining hand of God; it would immediately burst forth upon you. The sovereign pleasure of God, for the present, stays his rough wind; otherwise it would come with fury, and your destruction would come like a whirlwind, and you would be like the chaff of the summer threshing floor.

The wrath of God is like great waters that are dammed for the present; they increase more and more, and rise higher and higher, till an outlet is given; and the longer the stream is stopped, the more rapid and mighty is its course, when once it is let loose. It is true, that judgement against your evil works has not been executed hitherto; the floods of God's vengeance have been withheld; but your guilt in the meantime is constantly increasing, and you are every day treasuring up more wrath; the waters are constantly rising, and waxing more and more mighty;

and there is nothing but the mere pleasure of God, that holds the waters back, that are unwilling to be stopped, and press hard to go forward. If God should only withdraw his hand from the flood-gate, it would immediately fly open, and the fiery floods of the fierceness and wrath of God, would rush forth with inconceivable fury, and would come upon you with omnipotent power; and if your strength were ten thousand times greater than it is, yea, ten thousand times greater than the strength of the stoutest, sturdiest devil in hell, it would be nothing to withstand or endure it.

The bow of God's wrath is bent, and the arrow made ready on the string, and justice bends the arrow at your heart, and strains the bow, and it is nothing but the mere pleasure of God, and that of an angry God, without any promise or obligation at all, that keeps the arrow one moment from being made drunk with your blood. Thus all you that never passed under a great change of heart, by the mighty power of the Spirit of God upon your souls; all you that were never born again, and made new creatures, and raised from being dead in sin, to a state of new, and before altogether unexperienced light and life, are in the hands of an angry God.

However you may have reformed your life in many things, and may have had religious affections, and may keep up a form of religion in your families and closets, and in the house of God, it is nothing but his mere pleasure that keeps you from being this moment swallowed up in everlasting destruction. However unconvinced you may now be of the truth of what you hear, by and by you will be fully convinced of it. Those that are gone from being in the like circumstances with you, see that it was so with them; for destruction came suddenly upon most of them; when they expected nothing of it, and while they were saying, Peace and safety: Now they see, that those things on which they depended for peace and safety, were nothing but thin air and empty shadows.

The God that holds you over the pit of hell, much as one holds a spider, or some loathsome insect over the fire, abhors you, and is dreadfully provoked; his wrath towards you burns like fire; he looks upon you as worthy of nothing else, but to be cast into the fire; he is of purer eyes than to bear to have you in his sight; you are ten thousand times more abominable in his eyes, than the most hateful venomous serpent is in ours. You have offended him infinitely more than ever a stubborn rebel did his prince; and yet it is nothing but his hand that holds you from falling into the fire every moment.

It is to be ascribed to nothing else, that you did not go to hell the last night; that you was suffered to awake again in this world, after you closed your eyes to sleep. And there is no other reason to be given, why you have not dropped into hell since you arose in the morning, but that God's hand has held you up. There is no other reason to be given why you have not gone to hell, since you have sat here in the house of God, provoking his pure eyes by your sinful wicked manner of attending his solemn worship. Yea, there is nothing else that is to be given as a reason why you do not this very moment drop down into hell.

O sinner! Consider the fearful danger you are in; it is a great furnace of wrath, a wide and bottomless pit, full of the fire of wrath, that you are held over in the hand of that God, whose wrath is provoked and incensed as much against you, as against many of the damned in hell. You hang by a slender thread, with the flames of divine wrath flashing about it, and ready every moment to singe it, and burn it asunder; and you have no interest in any Mediator, and nothing to lay hold of to save yourself, nothing to keep off the flames of wrath, nothing of your own, nothing that you ever have done, nothing that you can do, to induce God to spare you one moment.

★   ★   ★

And consider here more particularly:

Whose wrath it is; it is the wrath of the infinite God. If it were only the wrath of man, though it were of the most potent prince, it would be comparatively little to be regarded. The wrath of kings is very much dreaded, especially of absolute monarchs, who have the possessions and lives of their subject wholly in their power, to be disposed of at their mere will. (Proverbs, chapter 20, verse 2) 'The fear of a king is as the roaring of a lion; Whose provoketh him to anger, sinneth against his own soul.' The subject that very much enrages an arbitrary prince, is liable to suffer the most extreme torments that human art can invent, or human power can inflict. But the greatest earthly potentates in their greatest majesty and strength, and when clothed in their greatest terrors, are but feeble, despicable worms of the dust, in comparison of the great and almighty Creator and King of heaven and earth. It is but little that they can do, when most enraged, and when they have exerted the utmost of their fury. All the kings of the earth, before God, are as grasshoppers; they are nothing, and less than nothing: both their love and their hatred is to be despised. The wrath of the great King of kings, is as much more terrible than theirs, as his majesty is greater. (Luke, chapter 12, verse 4): 'And I say unto you, my friends, Be not afraid of them that kill the body, and after that, have no more that they can do. But I will forewarn you whom you shall fear: fear him, which after hath killed, hath power to cast into hell; yea, I say unto you, Fear him.'

★   ★   ★

It is the *fierceness* of his wrath that you are exposed to. We often read of the fury of God: 'According to their deeds, accordingly he will repay fury to his adversaries.' So Isaiah, chapter 66, verse 15: 'For behold, the Lord will come with fire, and with his chariots like a whirlwind to render his anger with fury, and his rebuke with flames of fire.' And in many other places. So, (Revelation, chapter 19, verse 15) we read of 'the wine-press of the fierceness and wrath of Almighty God'. The words are exceeding terrible. If it had only been said, 'the wrath of God', the words would have implied that which is infinitely dreadful: but it is 'the fierceness and wrath of God'. The fury of God! The fierceness of Jehovah! Oh, how dreadful must that be! Who can utter or conceive what such expressions carry in them! But it is also 'the fierceness and wrath of *Almighty* God'. As though there would be a very great manifestation of his almighty power in what the fierceness of his wrath should inflict, as though omnipotence should be as it were enraged, and exerted, as men are wont to exert their strength in the fierceness of their wrath. *Oh!* then, what will be the consequence! What will become of the poor worm that shall suffer it! Whose hands can be strong? And whose heart can endure? To what a dreadful, inexpressible, inconceivable depth of misery must the poor creature be sunk who shall be the subject of this!

Consider this, you that are here present, that yet remain in an unregenerate state. That God will execute the fierceness of his anger, implies, that he will inflict wrath without any pity. When God beholds the ineffable extremity of your case, and sees your torment to be so vastly disproportioned to your strength, and sees how your poor soul is crushed, and sink down; as it were, into an infinite gloom; he will have no compassion upon you, he will not forbear the executions of his wrath, or in the least lighten his hand; there shall be no moderation of mercy, nor will God then at all stay his rough wind; he will have no regard to your welfare, nor be at all careful lest you should suffer too much in any other sense, than only that you shall *not suffer beyond what strict justice requires*. Nothing shall be withheld, because it is so hard for you to bear. (Ezekiel, chapter 8, verse 18): 'Therefore will I also deal in fury: mine eye shall not spare, neither will I have pity; and though they cry in mine ears with a loud voice, yet I will not hear them.'

Now God stands ready to pity you; this is a day of mercy; you may cry now with some encouragement of obtaining mercy. But when once the day of mercy is past, your most lamentable and dolorous cries and shrieks will be in vain; you will be wholly lost and thrown away of God, as to any regard to your welfare. God will have no other use to put you to, but to suffer misery; you shall be continued in being to no other end; for you will be a vessel of wrath fitted to destruction; and there will be no other use of this vessel, but to be filled full of wrath. God will be so far from pitying you when you cry to him, that it is said he will only 'laugh and mock' (Proverbs, chapter 1, verse 25).

How awful are those words, (Isaiah, chapter 63, verse 3) which are the words of the great God: 'I will tread them in mine anger, and will trample them in my fury, and their blood shall be sprinkled upon my garments, and I will stain all my raiment.' It is perhaps impossible to conceive of words that carry in them greater manifestations of these three things, viz: contempt, and hatred, and fierceness of indignation.

If you cry to God to pity you, he will be so far from pitying you in your doleful case, or shewing you the least regard or favour, that instead of that, he will only tread you under foot. And though he will know that you cannot bear the weight of omnipotence treading upon you, yet he will not regard that, but he will crush you under his feet without mercy; he will crush-out your blood, and make it fly, and it shall be sprinkled on his garments, so as to stain all his raiment. He will not only hate you, but he will have you in the utmost contempt; no place shall be thought fit for you, but under his feet to be trodden down as the mire of the streets . . .

★　　　★　　　★

And now you have an extraordinary opportunity, a day wherein Christ has thrown the door of mercy wide open, and stands in calling and crying with a loud voice to poor sinners; a day wherein many are flocking to him, and pressing into the kingdom of God. Many are daily coming from the east, west, north and south; many that were very lately in the same miserable condition that you are in, are now in a happy state, with their hearts filled with love to him who has loved them, and washed them from their sins in his own blood, and rejoicing in hope of the glory of God. How awful is it to be left behind at such a day! To see so many other feasting, while you are pining and perishing! To see so many rejoicing and singing for joy of heart, while you have cause to mourn for sorrow of heart, and howl for vexation of spirit! How can you rest one moment in such a condition? Are not your souls as precious as the souls of the people at Suffield, where they are flocking from day to day to Christ?

Are there not many here who have lived long in the world, and are not to this day born again? And so are aliens from the commonwealth of Israel, and have done nothing ever since they have lived, but treasure up wrath against the day of wrath? Oh, sirs, your case, in an especial manner, is extremely dangerous. Your guilt and hardness of heart is extremely great. Do you not see how generally persons of your years are passed over and left, in the present remarkable and wonderful dispensation of God's mercy? You had need to consider yourselves, and awake thoroughly out of sleep. You cannot bear the fierceness and wrath of the infinite God.

And you, young men, and young women, will you neglect this precious season which you now enjoy, when so many others of your age are renouncing all youthful vanities, and flocking to Christ? You especially have now an extraordinary opportunity; but if you neglect it, it will soon be with you as with those persons who spent all the precious days of youth in sin, and are now come to such a dreadful pass in blindness and hardness.

And you, children, who are unconverted, do not you know that you are going down to hell, to bear the dreadful wrath of that God, who is now angry with you every day and every night? Will you be content to be the children of the devil, when so many other children in the land are converted, and are become the holy and happy children of the King of kings?

And let every one that is yet out of Christ, and hanging over the pit of hell, whether they be old men and women, or middle aged, or young people, or little children, now hearken to the loud calls of God's word and providence. This acceptable year of the Lord, a day of such great favour to some, will doubtless be a day of as remarkable vengeance to others. Men's hearts harden, and their guilt increases apace at such a day as this, if they neglect their souls;

and never was there so great danger of such persons being given up to hardness of heart and blindness of mind.

God seems now to be hastily gathering in his elect in all parts of the land; and probably the greater part of adult persons that ever shall be saved, will be brought in now in a little time, and that it will be as it was on the great out-pouring of the Spirit upon the Jews in the apostles' days; the election will obtain and the rest will be blinded. If this should be the case with you, you will eternally curse this day, and will curse the day that ever you was born, to see such a season of the pouring out of God's Spirit, and will wish that you had died and gone to hell before you had seen it. Now undoubtedly it is, as it was in the days of John the Baptist, the axe is in an extraordinary manner laid at the root of the trees, that every tree which brings not forth good fruit, may be hewn down and cast into the fire.

Therefore, let every one that is out of Christ, now awake and fly from the wrath to come. The wrath of Almighty God is now undoubtedly hanging over a great part of this congregation: Let everyone fly out of Sodom: 'Haste and escape for your lives, look not behind you, escape to the mountain, lest you be consumed.'

A prayer found in
Mrs Chapone's handwriting after her death

O Gracious Father of the universe! behold thy creature humbly imploring thy forgiveness of her numerous past transgressions, and thy compassion for her present faulty dispositions, and her defects in all those virtues that must raise her to a better condition. Turn not from me, O my God, the light of thy countenance, nor take from me the blessed influence of thy spirit! – enlighten my under-standing – strengthen my faith – purify and invigorate the desires of my heart towards that which is good. Save and deliver me from evil, O Lord God most holy! most beneficent and merciful

Creator! consign me not to destruction – cast not me out from thy presence and the society of good spirits, but grant me all the assistance I stand in need of, to become what I ought to be, and to make the best use of that short period of life, which may still remain for me in this world.

Hester Chapone (1727–1801)

SERMON THIRTEEN

John Wesley

If John Wesley (1703–1791) invented a new Christian denomination –
Methodism – it must be remembered that he remained all his life a member
of the Church of England. The son of a clergyman, Wesley was educated
at Oxford University, and was elected a fellow of Lincoln College there. It
was at Oxford that he began to take his religion seriously. Throughout his
life he was open to wide influences, at first Jeremy Taylor, The Imitation
of Christ, *and then more deeply William Law's* Serious Call, *and the*
mysticism of Jacob Boehme. Moravianism was a later influence.

But Wesley followed his own path, shrugging off worldly mockery of
'Methodism'. His missionary journey with his brother Charles to Georgia
did not thrive, but on his return John Wesley felt, at a religious meeting,
assurance of salvation. He always rejected the Calvinism that his colleague
George Whitefield embraced. His earthly energy and tenacity urged him
on to set up a network of preachers in the open air or in any meeting house.
The Methodists looked to him to resolve all problems. He travelled
225,000 miles on horseback, preached 40,000 sermons, and left on his
death 70,000 Methodists in Britain, with another 60,000 in America.

'The Circumcision of the Heart' sounds a weird title to us today. It was
delivered on the day marking the Circumcision of Jesus, 1 January. A
sermon to the University, it shows that a year before his departure for
Georgia he was deeply committed to a religion of the heart that would
mean deeds of charity.

The circumcision of the heart

Preached at St Mary's, Oxford, before the University,
1 January 1733.

Circumcision is that of the heart, in the spirit, and not in the
letter. (Romans 2:29)

First: It is the melancholy remark of an excellent man, that he who
now preaches the most essential duties of Christianity, runs the
hazard of being esteemed, by a great part of his hearers, 'a setter

forth of new doctrines'. Most men have so lived away the substance of that religion the profession whereof they still retain, that no sooner are any of those truths proposed which difference the Spirit of Christ from the spirit of the world, than they cry out, 'Thou bringest strange things to our ears; we would know what these things mean': – though he is only preaching to them 'Jesus and the resurrection', with the necessary consequence of it – If Christ be risen, ye ought then to die unto the world, and to live wholly unto God.

Second: A hard saying this to the natural man, who is alive unto the world, and dead unto God; and one that he will not readily be persuaded to receive as the truth of God, unless it be so qualified in the interpretation, as to have neither use nor significancy left. He 'receiveth not the' words 'of the Spirit of God', taken in their plain and obvious meaning; 'they are foolishness unto him: Neither' indeed 'can he know them, because they are spiritually discerned': – They are perceivable only by that spiritual sense, which in him was never yet awakened; for want of which he must reject, as idle fancies of men, what are both the wisdom and the power of God.

Third: That 'circumcision is that of the heart, in the spirit, and not in the letter' – that the distinguishing mark of a true follower of Christ, of one who is in a state of acceptance with God, is not either outward circumcision, or baptism, or any other outward form, but a right state of soul, a mind and spirit renewed after the image of Him that created it – is one of those important truths that can only be spiritually discerned. And this the Apostle himself intimates in the next words – 'Whose praise is not of men, but of God.' As if he had said, 'Expect not, whoever thou art, who thus followest thy great Master, that the world, the men who follow him not, will say, "Well done, good and faithful servant!" Know that the circumcision of the heart, the seal of thy calling, is foolishness with the world. Be content to wait for thy applause till the day of thy Lord's appearing. In that day shalt thou have praise of God, in the great assembly of men and angels.'

I design particularly to inquire, wherein this circumcision of the heart consists.

★   ★   ★

I am, first, to inquire, wherein that circumcision of the heart consists, which will receive the praise of God. In general we may observe, it is that habitual disposition of soul which, in the sacred writings, is termed holiness; and which directly implies, the being cleansed from sin, 'from all filthiness both of flesh and spirit'; and, by consequence, the being endued with those virtues which were also in Christ Jesus; the being so 'renewed in the spirit of our mind', as to be 'perfect as our Father in heaven is perfect'.

Second: To be more particular: Circumcision of heart implies humility, faith, hope, and charity. Humility, a right judgement of ourselves, cleanses our minds from those high conceits of our own perfections, from that undue opinion of our own abilities and attainments, which are the genuine fruit of a corrupted nature.

This entirely cuts off that vain thought, 'I am rich, and wise, and have need of nothing'; and convinces us that we are by nature 'wretched, and poor, and miserable, and blind, and naked'. It convinces us, that in our best estate we are, of ourselves, all sin and vanity; that confusion, and ignorance, and error reign over our understanding; that unreasonable, earthly, sensual, devilish passions usurp authority over our will; in a word, that there is no whole part in our soul, that all the foundations of our nature are out of course.

Third: At the same time we are convinced, that we are not sufficient of ourselves to help ourselves; that, without the Spirit of God, we can do nothing but add sin to sin; that it is He alone who worketh in us by His almighty power, either to will or do that which is good; it being as impossible for us even to think a good thought, without the supernatural assistance once of His Spirit, as to create ourselves, or to renew our whole souls in righteousness and true holiness.

Fourth: A sure effect of our having formed this right judgement of the sinfulness arid helplessness of our nature, is a disregard of that 'honour which cometh of man' which is usually paid to some supposed excellency in us. He who knows himself, neither desires nor values the applause which he knows he deserves not. It is therefore 'a very small thing with him, to be judged by man's judgement'. He has all reason to think, by comparing what it has said, either for or against him, with what he feels in his own breast, that the world, as well as the god of this world, was 'a liar from the beginning'. And even as to those who are not of the world; though he would choose, if it were the will of God, that they should account of him as of one desirous to be found a faithful steward of his Lord's goods, if haply this might be a means of enabling him to be of more use to his fellow-servants, yet as this is the one end of his wishing for their approbation, so he does not at all rest upon it: For he is assured, that whatever God wills, he can never want instruments to perform; since he is able, even of these stones, to raise up servants to do his pleasure.

Fifth: This is that lowliness of mind, which they have learned of Christ, who follow his example and tread in his step. And this knowledge of their disease, whereby they are more and more cleansed from one part of it, pride arid vanity, disposes them to embrace, with a willing mind, the second thing implied in cir-cumcision of the heart – that faith which alone is able to make them whole, which is the one medicine given under heaven to heal their sickness.

Sixth: The best guide of the blind, the surest light of them that are in darkness, the most perfect instructor of the foolish, is faith. But it must be such a faith as is 'mighty through God, to the pulling down of strong-holds', to the over-turning all the preju-dices of corrupt reason, all the false maxims revered among men, all evil customs and habits, all that 'wisdom of the world which is foolishness with God'; as 'casteth down imaginations', reasonings, 'and every high thing that exalteth itself against the knowledge of God, and bring into captivity every thought to the obedience of Christ'.

Seventh: 'All things are possible to him that' thus 'believeth'. 'The eyes of his understanding being enlightened', he sees what is his calling; even to glorify God, who hath bought him with so high a price, in his body and in his spirit, which now are God's by redemption, as well as by creation. He feels what is 'the exceeding greatness of his power', who, as he raised up Christ from the dead, so is able to quicken us, dead in sin, 'by his Spirit which dwelleth in us'. 'This is the victory which overcometh the world, even our faith'; that faith, which is not only an unshaken assent to all that God hath revealed in Scripture – in particular to those important truths, 'Jesus Christ came into the world to save sinners'; 'He bore our sins in his own body on the tree'; 'He is the propitiation for our sins, and not for ours only, but also for the sins of the whole world.'

Eighth: Such a faith as this cannot fit to show evidently the power of Him that inspires it, by delivering His children from the yoke of sin, and 'purging their consciences from dead works'; by strengthening them so, that they are no longer constrained to obey sin in the desires thereof; but instead of 'yielding their members unto it, as instruments of unrighteousness', they now 'yield themselves' entirely 'unto God, as those that are alive from the dead'.

Ninth: Those who are thus by faith born of God, have also strong consolation through hope. This is the next thing which the circumcision of the heart implies; even the testimony of their own spirit with the Spirit which witnesses in their hearts that they are the children of God. Indeed it is the same Spirit who works in them that clear and cheerful confidence that their heart is upright toward God; that good assurance, that they now do, through his grace, the things which are acceptable in his sight; that they are new in the path which leadeth to life, and shall, by the mercy of God, endure therein to the end. It is He who giveth them a lively expectation of receiving all good things at God's hand; a joyous prospect of that crown of glory, which is reserved in heaven for them. By this anchor a Christian is kept steady in the midst of the waves of this troublesome world, and preserved from striking upon either of those fatal rocks – presumption or despair.

He is neither discouraged by the misconceived severity of his Lord, nor does he 'despise the riches of his goodness'. He neither apprehends the difficulties of the race set before him to be greater than he has strength to conquer, nor expects them to be so little as to yield in the conquest, till he has put forth all his strength. The experience he already has in the Christian warfare, as it assures him his 'labour is not in vain', if 'whatever his hand findeth to do, he doeth it with his might'; so it forbids his entertaining so vain a thought, as that he can otherwise gain any advantage, as that any virtue can be shown, any praise attained, by faint hearts and feeble hands; or, indeed, by any but those who pursue the same course with the great Apostle of the Gentiles: 'I', says he, 'so run, not as uncertainly; so fight I, not as one that beateth the air: But I keep under my body, and bring it into subjection; lest, by any means, when I have preached to others, I myself should be a castaway.'

Tenth: By the same discipline is every good soldier of Christ to inure himself to endure hardship. Confirmed and strengthened by this, he will be able not only to renounce the works of darkness, but every appetite too, and every affection, which is not subject to the law of God. For 'every one', saith St John, 'who hath this hope, purifieth himself even as He is pure'. It is his daily care, by the grace of God in Christ, and through the blood of the covenant, to purge the inmost recesses of his soul from the lusts that before possessed and defiled it; from un-cleanness, and envy, and malice, and wrath; from every passion and temper that is after the flesh, that either springs from or cherishes his native corruption: As well knowing, that he whose very body is the temple of God, ought to admit into it nothing common or unclean; and that holiness becometh that house for ever, where the Spirit of holiness vouchsafes to dwell.

Eleventh: Yet lackest thou one thing, whosoever thou art, that to a deep humility, and a steadfast faith, hast joined a lively hope, and thereby in a good measure cleansed thy heart from its inbred pollution. If thou wilt be perfect, add to all these, charity; add love, and thou best the circumcision of the heart, 'Love is the fulfilling of the law, the end of the commandment.'

Very excellent things are spoken of love; it is the essence, the spirit, the life of all virtue. It is not only the first and great command, but it is all the commandments in one. 'Whatsoever things are just, whatsoever things are pure, whatsoever things are amiable', or honourable; 'if there be any virtue, if there be any praise', they are all comprised in this one word – love. In this is perfection, and glory, and happiness. The royal law of heaven and earth is this, 'Thou shalt love the Lord thy God with all thy heart, and with all thy will, and with all thy mind, and with all thy strength.'

Twelfth: Not that this forbids us to love anything besides God: It implies that we love our brother also. Nor yet does it forbid us (as some have strangely imagined) to take pleasure in anything but God. To suppose this, is to suppose the Fountain of holiness is directly the author of sin; since he has inseparably annexed pleasure to the use of those creatures which are necessary to sustain the life he has given us. This, therefore, can never be the meaning of his command.

What the real sense of it is, both our blessed Lord and his Apostles tell us too frequently and too plainly, to be misunderstood. They all with one mouth bear witness, that the true meaning of those several declarations – 'The Lord thy God is one Lord'; 'Thou shalt have no other gods but me'; 'Thou shalt love the Lord thy God with all thy strength'; 'Thou shalt cleave unto him'; 'The desire of thy soul shall be to his name' – is no other than this: The one perfect Good shall be your one ultimate end. One thing shall ye desire for its own sake – the fruition of Him that is All in all.

One happiness shall ye propose to your souls, even an union with Him that made them; the having 'fellowship with the Father and the Son'; the being joined to the Lord in one Spirit. One design you are to pursue to the end of time – the enjoyment of God in time and in eternity. Desire other things, so far as they tend to this. Love the creature as it leads to the Creator. But in every step you take, be this the glorious point that terminates your view. Let every affection, and thought, and word, and work, be subordinate to this. Whatever ye desire or fear, whatever ye seek or shun, whatever ye think, speak, or do, be it in order to your happiness in God, the sole End, as well as Source, of your being.

Thirteenth: Have no end, no ultimate end, but God. Thus our Lord: 'One thing is needful': And if thine eye be singly, fixed on this one thing, 'thy whole body shall be full of light'. Thus St Paul: 'This one thing I do; I press toward the mark, for the prize of the high calling in Christ Jesus.' Thus St James: 'Cleanse your hands, ye sinners, and purify your hearts, ye double-minded.' Thus St John: 'Love not the world, neither the things that are in the world. For all that is in the world, the lust of the flesh, the lust of the eye, and the pride of life, is not of the Father, but is of the world.' The seeking happiness in what gratifies either the desire of the flesh, by agreeably striking upon the outward senses; the desire of the eye, of the imagination, by its novelty, greatness, or beauty; or the pride of life, whether by pomp, grandeur, power, or, the usual consequence of them, applause and admiration – 'is not of the Father', cometh not from, neither is approved by, the Father of spirits; 'but of the world': It is the distinguishing mark of those who will not have Him to reign over them.

A prayer that may be daily said by a woman in the state of pregnancy

O Lord God Almighty, Creator of heaven and earth, preserve, I beseech thee, the work of thy hands; and defend both me and the tender fruit of my womb from all perils and all evils. Grant me in due time a happy delivery and bring my child safe to the font of baptism, that it may be there happily dedicated to thee, to love and serve thee faithfully for ever. Through Jesus Christ thy Son our Lord. Amen

Richard Challoner (1691–1781)
From *The Garden of the Soul*

SERMON FOURTEEN

Laurence Sterne

Laurence Sterne (1713–1768) made his name in 1759 with the first two volumes of the novel Tristram Shandy, *a comic modernist masterpiece. He added volumes annually until his death. The parson in the novel was called Yorick, and it was under this persona that Sterne published his own sermons. They are of their time, quizzical, humane, unzealous. Sterne took his own mortal sickness lightly and hoped for the best from an understanding and reasonable God.*

Evil speaking

If any man among you seem to be religious, and bridleth not his tongue, but deceiveth his own heart, that man's religion is vain. (James 1:26)

Of the many duties owing both to God and our neighbour, there are scarce any men so bad, as not to acquit themselves of some, and few so good, I fear, as to practise all.

Every man seems willing enough to compound the matter, and adopt so much of the system as will least interfere with his principal and ruling passion, and for those parts which would occasion a more troublesome opposition, to consider them as hard sayings, and so leave them for those to practise, whose natural tempers are better suited to the struggle. So that a man shall be covetous, oppressive, revengeful, neither a lover of truth, or common honesty, and yet at the same time, shall be *very* religious, and so sanctified, as not once to fail of paying his morning and evening sacrifice to God.

So, on the other hand, a man shall live without God in the world, have neither any great sense of religion, or indeed pretend to have any, and yet be of nicest honour, conscientiously just and fair in all his dealings. And here it is that men generally betray themselves, deceiving, as the apostle says, their own hearts; of which the instances are so various, in one degree or other throughout human life, that one might safely say, the bulk of mankind live in such a contradiction to themselves, that there is no character so hard to be met with as one which upon a critical examination will appear altogether uniform, and in every point consistent with itself.

If such a contrast was only observable in the different stages of man's life, it would cease to be either a matter of wonder or of just reproach. Age, experience, and much reflection, may naturally enough be supposed to alter a man's sense of things, and so entirely to transform him, that not only in outward appearances, but in the very cast and turn of his mind, he may be as unlike and different from the man he was twenty or thirty years ago, as he ever was from any thing of his own species.

This, I say, is naturally to be accounted for, and in some cases might be praiseworthy too; but the observation is to be made of men in the same period of their lives, that in the same day, sometimes in the very same action, they are utterly inconsistent and irreconcileable with themselves.

Look at a man in one light, and he shall seem wise, penetrating, discreet and brave: behold him in another point of view, and you see a creature all over folly and indiscretion, weak and timorous, as cowardice and indiscretion can make him. A man shall appear gentle, courteous and benevolent to all mankind; follow him into his own house, may be you see a tyrant, morose and savage to all whole happiness depends upon his kindness. A third in his general behaviour is found to be generous, disinterested, humane, and friendly – hear but the sad story of the friendless orphans, too credulously trusting all their little substance into his hands, and he shall appear more sordid, more pitiless and unjust, than the injured themselves have bitterness to paint him.

Another shall be charitable to the poor, uncharitable in his censures and opinions of all the rest of the world besides – temperate in his appetites, intemperate in his tongue; shall have too much conscience and religion to cheat the man who trusts him, and perhaps, as far as the business of debtor and creditor extends, shall be just and scrupulous to the uttermost mite; yet in matters of full as great concern, where he is to have the handling of the party's reputation and good name – the dearest, the tenderest property the man has – he will do him irreparable damage, and rob him there without measure or pity.

And this seems to be that particular piece of inconsistency and contradiction which the text is levelled at, in which the words seem so pointed, as if St James had known more flagrant instances of this kind of delusion than what had fallen under the observation of any of the rest of the apostles; he being more remarkably vehement and copious upon the subject than any other.

Doubtless some of his converts had been notoriously wicked and licentious in this remorseless practice of defamation and evil-speaking. Perhaps the holy man, though spotless as an angel, (for no character is too sacred for calumny to blacken), had grieviously suffered himself, and as his blessed master foretold him, had been cruelly reviled and evil *spoken* of.

All his labours in the gospel, his unaffected and perpetual solicitude for the preservation of his flock, his watchings and fastings, his natural simplicity and innocence of life – *all* perhaps were not enough to defend him from this unruly weapon, so full of deadly poison. And what in all likelihood might move his sorrow and indignation more, one who seemed the most devout and zealous of all his converts, were the most merciless and uncharitable in the respect: Having a form of godliness, full of bitter envyings and strife.

With such it is, that he expostulates so largely in the third chapter of his epistle; and there is something in his vivacity, tempered with such affection, and concern, as well suited the character of an inspired man. My brethren, says the apostle, these things ought not to be. – The wisdom that is from above is pure, peaceable, gentle, full of mercy, without partiality, without hypocrisy. The wisdom from above – that heavenly religion which I have preached to you, is pure, alike and consistent with itself in all its parts; like its great Author, 'tis universally kind and benevolent in all cases and circumstances. Its first glad tidings, were peace upon earth, good-will towards men; its chief corner-stone, its most distinguishing character is *love*, that kind principle which brought it down, in the pure exercise of which consists the chief enjoyment of heaven from whence it came.

But this practice, my brethren, cometh not from above, but it is earthly, sensual, devilish, full of confusion and every evil work. Reflect then a moment; can a fountain send forth at the same place, sweet water and bitter? Can the fig-tree, my brethren, bear olive berries; or a vine, figs. Lay your hands upon your hearts, and let your consciences speak. – Ought not the same just principle, which restrains you from cruelty and wrong in one case, equally to withhold you from it in another? – Should not charity and good will, like the principle of life, circulating through the smallest vessels in every member, ought it not to operate as regularly upon you, throughout, as well upon your words as upon your actions?

If a man is wise and endued with knowledge, let him shew it, out of a good conversation, with meekness of wisdom. But – if any man amongst you seemeth to be religious – seemeth to be – for truly religious he cannot be – and bridleth not his tongue, but deceiveth his own heart, this man's religion is vain. – This is the full force of St James's reasoning; upon which I have dwelt the more, it being the foundation, upon which is grounded this clear decision of the matter left us in the text. In which the apostle seems to have set the two characters of a saint and a slanderer at such variance, that one would have thought they could never have had a heart to have met together again. But there are no alliances too strange for this world. – How many may we observe every day, even of the gentler sex, as well as our own, who without conviction of doing much wrong in the midst of a full career of calumny and defamation, rise up punctually at the stated hour of prayer, leave the cruel story half untold till they return, – go – and kneel down before the throne of heaven, thank God that he had not made them like others, and that his Holy Spirit had enabled them to perform the duties of the day, in so christian and conscientious a manner? . . .

★   ★   ★

We all cry out that the world is corrupt – and I fear too justly – but we never reflect, what we have to thank for it, and that our open countenance of vice, which gives the lye to our private censures of it, is its chief protection and encouragement. – To those however, who still believe that evil-speaking is some terror to evil-doers, one may answer, as a great man has done upon the occasion – that after all our exhortations against it – 'tis not to be feared, but that there will be evil-speaking enough left in the world to chastise the guilty – and we may safely trust them to an ill-natured world, that there will be no failure of justice upon this score. – The passions of men are pretty severe executioners, and to them let us leave this ungrateful talk – and rather ourselves endeavour to cultivate that more friendly one, recommended by the apostle – of letting all bitterness, and wrath, and clamour, and evil-speaking, be put away from us – of being kind to one another – tender-hearted, forgiving one another, even as God for Christ's sake forgave us. Amen.

Hymn

Gentle Jesus, meek and mild,
Look upon a little child;
Pity my simplicity,
Suffer me to come to thee.

Fain I would to thee be brought:
Dearest God, forbid it not;
Give me, blessed Lord, a place
In the kingdom of thy grace.

Charles Wesley (1707–1788)

Charles Wesley wrote more than 5,000 hymns.

SERMON FIFTEEN

❦

Sydney Smith

Sydney Smith (1771–1845) had a reputation as a wit that was not unearned. He was ordained a parson in the Church of England in his early twenties in the conventional way after taking his degree at Oxford and being elected a fellow of New College there. But he had a heart, and a disgust with cant, that gave his sermons an original appeal. As a founder of the Edinburgh Review *he was able to criticize with impatient humour the perpetrators of dull, unthinking, clichéd sermons. He was tolerant of religious underdogs such as the Catholics in the Britain of his time, but intolerant of aggressively held dogma. The Book of Common Prayer in his day, and up to the mid-nineteenth century, included a service for 5 November, to mark the sparing of the King in Parliament from being blown up in 1605.*

The rules of Christian charity

Put on, as the elect of god, kindness, humbleness of mind, meekness, long-suffering, forbearing one another, and forgiving one another. (Colossians 3:12)

The Church of England, in its wisdom and piety, has very properly ordained that a day of thanksgiving should be set apart, in which we may return thanks to Almighty God, for the mercies vouchsafed to this nation in their escape from the dreadful plot planned for the destruction of the Sovereign and his Parliament – the forerunner, no doubt, of such sanguinary scenes as were suited to the manners of that age, and most have proved the inevitable consequence of such enormous wickedness and cruelty. Such an escape is a fair and lawful foundation for national piety. And it is a comely and Christian sight to see the magistrates and high authorities of the land obedient to the ordinances of the Church, and holding forth to their fellow subjects a wise example of national gratitude and serious devotion. This use of this day is deserving of every commendation. The idea that Almighty God does sometimes exercise a special providence for the preservation of a whole people is justified by Scripture, is not repugnant to reason, and can produce nothing but feelings and opinions favourable to virtue and religion.

Another wise and lawful use of this day is an honest self-congratulation that we have burst through those bands which the Roman Catholic priesthood would impose upon human judgement; that the Protestant Church not only permits, but exhorts, every man to appeal from human authority to the Scriptures; that it makes of the clergy guides and advisers, not masters and oracles; that it discourages vain and idle ceremonies, unmeaning observances, and hypocritical pomp; and encourages freedom in thinking upon religion, and simplicity in religious forms. It is impossible that any candid man should not observe the marked superiority of the Protestant over the Catholic faith in these particulars; and difficult that any pious man should not feel grateful to Almighty Providence for escape from danger which would have plunged this country afresh into so many errors and so many absurdities.

I hope in this condemnation of the Catholic religion (in which I most sincerely join its bitterest enemies), I shall not be so far mistaken as to have it supposed that I would convey the slightest approbation of any laws which disqualify or incapacitate any class of men from civil offices on account of religious opinions. I regard all such laws as fatal and lamentable mistakes in legislation; they are mistakes of troubled times, and half-barbarous ages. All Europe is gradually emerging from their influence. This country has lately, with the entire consent of its Prelates, made a noble and successful effort, by the abolition of some of the most obnoxious laws of this class. In proportion as such example is followed, the enemies of Church and State will be diminished, and the foundation of peace, order, and happiness be strengthened. These are but opinions, which I mention, not to convert you, but to guard myself from misrepresentation. It is my duty – it is my wish – it is the subject of this day to point out those evils of the Catholic religion from which we have escaped; but I should be to the last degree concerned, if a condemnation of theological errors were to be construed into an approbation of laws, which I cannot but consider as deeply marked by a spirit of intolerance.

I, therefore, beg you to remember that I record these opinions not for the purpose of converting any one to them, which would be an abuse of the privilege of addressing you from the pulpit; not that I attach the slightest degree of importance to them because they are mine; but merely to guard myself from misrepresentation upon a point on which all men's passions are, at this moment, so powerfully excited.

I have said that, at this moment, all men's passions are powerfully excited on this subject. If this is true, it points out to me my line of duty. I must use my endeavours to guard against the abuse of this day; to take care that the principles of sound reason are not lost sight of; and that such excitement, instead of rising into dangerous vehemence, is calmed into active and useful investigation of the subject.

I shall, therefore, on the present occasion, not investigate generally the duties of charity and forbearance, but of charity and forbearance in religious matters; of that Christian meekness and humility which prevent the intrusion of bad passions into religious concerns, and keep calm and pure the mind intent upon eternity. And remember, I beg of you, that the rules I shall offer you for the observation of Christian charity are general, and of universal application. What you choose to do, and which way you incline upon any particular question, are, and can be, no concern of mine. It would be the height of arrogance and presumption in me, or in any other minister of God's word, to interfere on such points; I only endeavour to teach that spirit of forbearance and charity, which (though it cannot always prevent differences upon religious points), will ensure that these differences are carried on with Christian gentleness. I have endeavoured to lay down these rules for difference with care and moderation; and, if you will attend to them patiently, I think you will agree with me, that however the practice of them may be forgotten, the propriety of them cannot be denied.

It would always be easier to fall in with human passions than to resist them; but the ministers of God must do their duty through evil report, and through good report; neither prevented nor excited by the interests of the present day. They must teach those general truths which the Christian religion has committed to their care, and, upon which the happiness and peace of the world depend.

In pressing upon you the great duty of religious charity, the inutility of the opposite defect of religious violence first offers itself to, and indeed obtrudes itself upon my notice. The evil of difference of opinion must exist – it admits of no cure. The wildest visionary does not now hope he can bring his fellow creatures to one standard of faith. If history has taught us any one thing, it is that mankind, on such sort of subjects, will form their own opinions. Therefore to want charity in religious matters is at least useless; it hardens error and provokes recrimination; but it does not enlighten those whom we wish to reclaim, nor does it extend doctrines which to us appear so clear and indisputable. But to do wrong, and to gain nothing by it, is surely to add folly to fault, and to proclaim an understanding not led by the rule of reason, as well as a disposition unregulated by the Christian faith.

Religious charity requires that we should not judge any sect of Christians by the representations of their enemies alone, without hearing and reading what they have to say in their own defence; it requires only, of course, to state such a rule to procure for it general admission. No man can pretend to say that such a rule is not founded upon the plainest principles of justice – upon those plain principles of justice which no one thinks of violating in the ordinary concerns of life; and yet I fear that rule is not always very strictly adhered to in religious animosities. Religious hatred is often founded on tradition, often on hearsay, often on the misrepresentations of notorious enemies; without inquiry, without the slightest examination of opposite reasons and authorities, or consideration of that which the accused party has to offer for defence or explanation. It is impossible, I admit, to examine every thing; many have not talents, many have not leisure, for such pursuits; many must be contented with the faith in which they have been brought up, and must think it the best modification of the Christian faith, because they are told it is so. But this imperfect acquaintance with religious controversy, though not blameable when it proceeds from want of power, and want of opportunity, can be no possible justification of violent and acrimonious opinions. I would say to the ignorant man, 'It is not your ignorance I blame; you have had no means perhaps of acquiring knowledge: the circumstances of your life have not led to it – may have prevented it; but then I must tell you, if you have not had leisure to inquire, you have no right to accuse. If you are unacquainted with the opposite arguments – or, knowing, cannot balance them, it is not upon you the task devolves of exposing the errors, and impugning the opinions of other sects.'

If charity is ever necessary, it is in those who know accurately neither the accusation nor the defence. If invective – if rooted antipathy, in religious opinions, is ever a breach of Christian rules, it is so in those who, not being able to become wise, are not willing to become charitable and modest.

Any candid man acquainted with religious controversy, will, I think, admit that he has frequently, in the course of his studies, been astonished by the force of arguments with which that cause has been defended, which he at first thought to be incapable of any defence at all. Some accusations he has found to be utterly groundless; in others the facts and arguments have been misstated; in other instances the accusation has been retorted: in many cases the tenets have been defended by strong arguments and honest appeal to Scripture, in many with consummate acuteness and deep learning. So that religious studies often teach to opponents a greater respect for each other's talents, motives, and acquirements; exhibit the real difficulties of the subject; lessen the surprise and anger which are apt to be excited by opposition; and, by these means, promote that forgiving one another, and forbearing one another which are so powerfully recommended by the words of my text.

A great deal of mischief is done by not attending to the limits of interference with each other's religious opinions – by not leaving to the power and wisdom of God, that which belongs to God alone. Our holy religion consists of some doctrines which influence practice, and of others which are purely speculative. If religious errors are of the former description, they may, perhaps, be fair objects of human interference; but, if the opinion is merely theological and speculative, there the right of human interference seems to end, because the necessity for such interference does not exist. Any error of this nature is between the Creator and the creature – between the Redeemer, and the redeemed.

If such opinions are not the best opinions which can he found, God Almighty will punish the error, if mere error seemeth to the Almighty a fit object of punishment. Why may not man wait if God waits? Where are we called upon in Scripture to pursue men for errors purely speculative? – to assist Heaven in punishing those offences which belong only to Heaven? – in fighting unasked for what we deem to be the battles of God – of that patient and merciful God, who pities the frailties we do not pity – who forgives the errors we do not forgive – who sends rain upon the just and the unjust, and maketh his sun to shine upon the evil and the good?

Another canon of religious charity is to revise, at long intervals, the bad opinions we have been compelled, or rather our fore-fathers have been compelled, to form of other Christian sects; to see whether the different bias of the age, the more general diffusion of intelligence, render those tenets less pernicious: that which prove a very great evil under other circumstances, and in other times, may perhaps, however weak and erroneous, be harmless in these times, and under these circumstances. We must be aware, too, that we do not mistake recollections for apprehensions, and confound together what has passed with what is to come – history with futurity. For instance, it would be the most enormous abuse of this religious institution to imagine that such dreadful scenes of wickedness are to be apprehended from the Catholics of the present day, because the annals of this country were disgraced by such an event two hundred years ago.

It would be an enormous abuse of this day to extend the crimes of a few desperate wretches to a whole sect; to fix the passions of dark ages upon times of refinement and civilization. All these are mistakes and abuses of this day, which violate every principle of Christian charity, endanger the peace of society, and give life and perpetuity to hatreds, which must perish at one time or another, and had better, for the peace of society, perish now.

It would be religiously charitable, also, to consider whether the objectionable tenets, which different sects profess, are in their hearts as well as in their books. There is unfortunately so much pride where there ought to be so much humility, that it is difficult, if not almost impossible, to make religious sects abjure or recant the doctrines they have once professed. It is not in this manner, I fear, that the best and purest churches are ever reformed. But the doctrine gradually becomes obsolete; and, though not disowned, ceases in fact to be a distinguishing characteristic of the sect which professes it.

These modes of reformation – this silent antiquation of doctrines – this real improvement, which the parties themselves are too wise not to feel, though not wise enough to own, must, I am afraid, be generally conceded to human infirmity. They are indulgences not unnecessary to many sects of Christians. The more generous method would be to admit error where error exists, to say these were the tenets and interpretations of dark and ignorant ages; wider inquiry, fresh discussion, superior intelligence have convinced us we are wrong; we will act in future upon better and wiser principles. This is what men do in laws, arts, and sciences; and happy for them would it be if they used the same modest docility in the highest of all concerns. But it is, I fear, more than experience will allow us to expect; and therefore the kindest and most charitable method is to allow religious sects silently to improve without reminding them of, and taunting them with, the improvement; without bringing them to the humiliation of formal disavowal, or the still more pernicious practice of defending what they know to be indefensible. The triumphs which proceed from the neglect of these principles are not (what they pretend to be) the triumphs of religion, but the triumphs of personal vanity. The object is not to extinguish dangerous error with as little pain and degradation as possible to him who has fallen into the error: but the object is to exalt ourselves, and to depreciate our theological opponents, as much as possible, at any expense to God's service, and to the real interests of truth and religion.

There is another practice not less common than this, and equally uncharitable; and that is to represent the opinions of the most violent and eager persons who can be met with, as the common and received opinions of the whole sect. There are, in every denomination of Christians, individuals, by whose opinion or by whose conduct the great body would very reluctantly be judged. Some men aim at attracting notice by singularity; some are deficient in temper; some in learning: some push every principle to the extreme; distort, overstate; pervert; fill everyone to whom their cause is dear with concern that it should have been committed to such rash and intemperate advocates. If you wish to gain a victory over your antagonists; these are the men whose writings you should study, whose opinions you should dwell on, and should carefully bring forward to notice; but if you wish, as the elect of God, to put on kindness and humbleness, meekness and long-suffering – if you, wish to forbear and to forgive, it will then occur to you that you should seek the true opinions of any sect from those only who are approved of, and reverenced by that sect; to whose authority that sect defer, and by whose arguments they consider their tenets to be properly defended. This may not suit your purpose if you are combating for victory; but it is your duty if you are combating for truth; it is safe, honest, and splendid conduct of him, who never writes nor speaks on religious subjects; but that he may diffuse the real blessings of religion among his fellow creatures, and restrain the bitterness of controversy by the feelings of Christian charity and forbearance.

Let us also ask ourselves, when we are sitting in severe judgement upon the faults, follies, and errors of other Christian sects, whether it is not barely possible that we have fallen into some mistakes and misrepresentations? Let us ask ourselves, honestly and fairly, whether we are wholly exempt from prejudice, from pride, from obstinate adhesion to what candour calls upon us to alter, and to yield? Are there no violent and mistaken members of our own community, by whose conduct we should he loath to be guided – by whose tenets we should not choose our faith should be judged? Has time, that improves all, found nothing in us to change for the better? Amid all the manifold divisions of the Christian world, are we the only Christians who, without having any thing to learn from the knowledge and civilization of the last three centuries, have started up, without infancy, and without error, into consummate wisdom and spotless perfection?

To listen to enemies as well as friends is a rule which not only increases sense in common life, but is highly favourable to the increase of religious candour. You find that you are not so free from faults as your friends suppose, nor so full of faults as your enemies suppose. You begin to think it not impossible that you may be as unjust to others as they are to you; and that the wisest and most Christian scheme is that of mutual indulgence; that it is better to put on, as the elect of God, kindness, humbleness of mind, meekness, long-suffering, forbearing one another, and forgiving one another.

Some men cannot understand how they are to be zealous if they are candid in religious matters; how the energy, necessary for the one virtue, is compatible with the calmness which the other requires. But remember that the Scriptures carefully distinguish between laudable zeal and indiscreet zeal; that the apostles and epistolary writers knew they had as much to fear from the over-excitement of some men, as from the supineness of others; and in nothing have they laboured more than in preventing religion from arming human passions instead of allaying them, and rendering those principles a source of mutual jealousy and hatred which were intended for universal peace.

I admit that indifference sometimes puts on the appearance of candour; but, though there is a counterfeit, yet there is a reality; and the imitation proves the value of the original, because men only attempt to multiply appearances of useful, and important things. The object is to be at the same time pious to God and charitable to man; to render your own faith as pure, and perfect as possible, not only without hatred of those who differ from you, but with a constant recollection that it is possible in spite of thought and study, that you may have been mistaken – that other sects may be right – and that a zeal in his service, which God does not want, is a very bad excuse for those bad passions which his sacred word condemns.

Lastly, I would suggest that many differences between sects are of less importance than the furious zeal of many men would make them. Are the tenets of any sect of such a description, that we believe they will be saved under the Christian faith? Do they fulfil the common duties of life? Do they respect property? Are they obedient to the laws? Do they speak the truth? If all these things are right, the violence of hostility may surely submit to some little softness and relaxation; honest difference of opinion cannot call for such entire separation and complete antipathy; such zeal as this, if it be zeal, and not something worse, is not surely zeal according to discretion . . .

★   ★   ★

I shall conclude my sermon, (pushed, I am afraid, already to an unreasonable length), by reciting to you a very short and beautiful apologue, taken from the Rabbinical writers. It is, I believe, quoted by Bishop Taylor in his *Holy Living and Dying*. I have not now access to that book, but I quote it to you from memory; and should be made truly happy if you would quote it to others from memory also.

'As Abraham was sitting in the door of his tent, there came unto him a wayfaring man; and Abraham gave him water for his feet, and set bread before him. And Abraham said unto him, "Let us now worship the Lord our God before we eat of this bread." And the wayfaring man said unto Abraham, "I will not worship the Lord thy God, for thy God is not my God; but I will worship my God, even the God of my fathers." But Abraham was exceeding wroth; and he rose up to put the wayfaring man forth from the door of his tent. And the voice of the Lord was heard in the tent – "Abraham, Abraham! have I borne with this man for three score and ten years, and canst not thou bear with him for one hour?"'

Gunpowder treason

Beneath the burning eastern sky
The Cross was rais'd at morn:
The widow'd Church to weep stood by,
The world to hate and scorn.

Now, journeying westward, evermore
We know the lonely Spouse
By the dear mark her Saviour bore
Trac'd on her patient brows.

At Rome she wears it, as of old
Upon th'accursed hill:
By monarchs clad in gems and gold,
She goes a mourner still.

She mourns that tender hearts should bend
Before a meaner shrine,
And upon Saint or Angel spend
The love that should be thine . . .

Speak gently of our sister's fall:
Who knows but gentle love
May win her at our patient call
The surer way to prove?

John Keble (1792–1866)
From *The Christian Year*

SERMON SIXTEEN

John Henry Newman

John Henry Newman changed the face of the Anglican Church, even though he left it halfway through his long life (1801–1890). He loved Oxford and while still in his twenties became Vicar of St Mary's, the University Church. He had tended to evangelicalism in his youth and took his priestly duties seriously. An attempt to represent the Church of England as part of the wider Catholic Church failed during Newman's long study of the ancient Fathers. In 1845, after writing his treatise on the Development of Christian Doctrine *he realized that he must become a Roman Catholic. As a founder of the Oratory in England he spent his life writing, exploring the concept of faith in* A Grammar of Assent, *examining the nature of dogma in* On Consulting the Laity *and* A Letter to the Duke of Norfolk. *His religious journey is told in the* Apologia *(1864), with its clear, nuanced prose style. He republished the sermons of his Anglican years with few amendments. 'Real', as opposed to theoretical or pretended, is one of the distinctions he liked to make; it was of a part with doing as well as saying. In this sermon, like Sterne, he looks at inconsistency in belief and behaviour.*

Promising without doing

A certain man had two sons; and he came to the first, and said, Son, go to work to-day in my vineyard. He answered and said, I will not; but afterward he repeated, and went. And he came to the second, and said likewise. And he answered and said, I go, Sir; and went not. (Matthew 21:28)

Our religious professions are at a far greater distance from our acting upon them, than we ourselves are aware. We know generally that it is our duty to serve God, and we resolve we will do so faithfully. We are sincere in thus generally desiring and purposing to be obedient, and we think we are in earnest; yet we go away, and presently, without any struggle of mind or apparent change of purpose, almost without knowing ourselves what we do – we go away and do the very contrary to the resolution we have expressed.

This inconsistency is exposed by our Blessed Lord in the second part of the parable which I have taken for my text. You will observe, that in the case of the first son, who said he would not go work, and yet did go, it is said, 'afterward he repented'; he underwent a positive change of purpose. But in the case of the second, it is merely said, 'he answered, I go, Sir; and went not' – for here there was *no* revolution of sentiment, nothing deliberate; he merely acted according to his habitual frame of mind; he did *not* work, because it was contrary to his general character to work; only he did not know this. He said, 'I go, Sir', sincerely, from the feeling of the moment; but when the words were out of his mouth, then they were forgotten. It was like the wind blowing against a stream, which seems for a moment to change its course in consequence, but in fact flows down as before.

To this subject I shall now call your attention, as drawn from the latter part of this parable, passing over the case of the repentant son, which would form a distinct subject in itself. 'He answered and said, I go, Sir; and went not.' We promise to serve God: we do not perform; and that not from deliberate faithlessness in the particular case, but because it is our nature, our *way* not to obey, and *we* do not know this; we do not know ourselves, or what we are promising. I will give several instances of this kind of weakness.

For instance; that of mistaking good feelings for real religious principle. Consider how often this takes place. It is the case with the young necessarily, who have not been exposed to temptation. They have (we will say) been brought up religiously, they wish to be religious, and so are objects of our love and interest; but they think themselves far more religious than they really are. They suppose they hate sin, and understand the Truth, and can resist the world, when they hardly know the meaning of the words they use.

Again, how often is a man incited by circumstances to utter a virtuous wish, or propose a generous or valiant deed, and perhaps applauds himself for his own good feeling, and has no suspicion that he is not able to act upon it! In truth, he does not understand where the real difficulty of his duty lies. He thinks that the characteristic of a religious man is his having correct notions. It escapes him that there is a great interval between feeling and acting. He takes it for granted he can do what he wishes. He knows he is a free agent, and can on the whole do what he will; but he is not conscious of the load of corrupt nature and sinful habits which hang upon his will, and clog it in each particular exercise of it. He has borne these so long, that he is insensible to their existence. He knows that in little things, where passion and inclination are excluded, he can perform as soon as he resolves. Should he meet in his walk two paths, to the right and left, he is sure he can take which he will at once, without any difficulty; and he fancies that obedience to God is not much more difficult than to turn to the right instead of the left.

One especial case of this self-deception is seen in delaying repentance. A man says to himself, 'Of course, if the worst comes to the worst, if illness comes, or at least old age, I can repent.' I do not speak of the dreadful presumption of such a mode of quieting conscience (though many persons really use it who do not speak the words out, or are aware that they act upon it), but, merely, of the ignorance it evidences concerning our moral condition, and our power of willing and doing. If men can repent, why do they not do so at once? They answer, that 'they intend to do so hereafter'; i.e. they do *not* repent because they *can*. Such is their argument; whereas, the very fact that they do not now, should make them suspect that there is a greater difference between intending and doing than they know of.

So very difficult is obedience, so hardly won is every step in our Christian course, so sluggish and inert our corrupt nature, that I would have a man disbelieve he can do one jot or tittle beyond what he has already done; refrain from borrowing aught on the hope of the future, however good a security for it he seems to be able to show; and never take his good feelings and wishes in pledge for one single untried deed. Nothing but *past* acts are the vouchers for *future*. Past sacrifices, past labours, past victories over yourselves – these, my brethren, are the tokens of the like in store, and doubtless of greater in store; for the path of the just is as the shining, growing light.

But trust nothing short of these. 'Deeds, not words and wishes', this must be the watchword of your warfare and the ground of your assurance. But if you have done nothing firm and manly hitherto, if you are as yet the coward slave of Satan, and the poor creature of your lusts and passions, never suppose you will one day rouse yourselves from your indolence. Alas! there are men who walk the road to hell, always the while looking back at heaven, and trembling as they pace forward towards their place of doom. They hasten on as under a spell, shrinking from the consequences of their own deliberate doings.

Such was Balaam. What would he have given if words and feelings might have passed for deeds! See how religious he was so far as profession goes! How did he revere God in speech! How piously express a desire to die the death of the righteous! Yet he died in battle among God's *enemies*; not suddenly overcome by temptation, only on the other hand, not suddenly turned to God by his good thoughts and fair purposes. But in this respect the power of sin differs from any literal spell or fascination, that we are, after all, willing slaves of it, and shall answer for following it. If 'our iniquities, like the wind, take us away', yet we can help this.

Nor is it only among beginners in religious obedience that there is this great interval between promising and performing. We can never answer how we shall act under new circumstances. A very little knowledge of life and of our own hearts will teach us this. Men whom we meet in the world turn out, in the course of their trial, so differently from what their former conduct promised, they view things so differently *before* they were tempted and *after*, that we, who see and wonder at it, have abundant cause to look to ourselves, not to be 'high-minded', but to 'fear'.

Even the most matured saints, those who imbibed in largest measure the power and fulness of Christ's Spirit, and worked righteousness most diligently in their day, could they have been thoroughly scanned even by man, would (I am persuaded) have exhibited inconsistencies such as to surprise and shock their most ardent disciples. After all, one good deed is scarcely the pledge of another, though I just now said it was. The best men are uncertain; they are great, and they are little again; they stand firm, and then fall. Such is human virtue – reminding us to call no one master on earth, but to look up to our sinless and perfect Lord; reminding us to humble ourselves, each within himself, and to reflect what we must appear to God, if even to ourselves and each other we seem so base and worthless; and showing clearly that all who are saved, even the least inconsistent of us, can be saved only by faith, not by works.

Here I am reminded of another plausible form of the same error. It is a mistake concerning what is meant by faith. We know Scripture tells us that God accepts those who have faith in Him. Now the question is, What *is* faith, and how can a man tell that he *has* faith? Some persons answer at once and without hesitation, that 'to have faith is to feel oneself to be nothing, and God every thing; it is to be convinced of sin, to be conscious one cannot save oneself, and to wish to be saved by Christ our Lord; and that it is, moreover, to have the love of Him warm in one's heart, and to rejoice in Him, to desire His glory, and resolve to live to Him and not to the world.'

But I will answer, with all due seriousness, as speaking on a serious subject, that this is *not* faith. Not that it is not necessary (it is very necessary) to be convinced that we are laden with infirmity and sin, and without health in us, and to look for Salvation solely to Christ's blessed sacrifice on the cross; and we may well be thankful if we are thus minded; but that a man may feel all this that I have described, vividly, and still not yet possess one particle of true religious faith. Why? Because there is an immeasurable distance between feeling right and doing right. A man may have all these good thoughts and emotions, yet (if he has not yet hazarded them to the experiment of practice) he cannot promise himself that he has any sound and permanent principle at all. If he has not yet acted upon them, we have no voucher, barely on *account* of them, to believe that they are any thing but words.

Though a man spoke like an angel, I would not believe him, on the mere ground of his speaking. Nay, till he acts upon them, he has not even evidence to himself that he has true living faith. Dead faith (as St James says) profits no man. Of course; the Devils have it. What, on the other hand is *living* faith? Do fervent thoughts make faith *living*? St James tells us otherwise. He tells us *works*, deeds of obedience, are the life of faith. 'As the body without the spirit is dead, so faith without works is dead also.' So that those who think they really believe, because they have in word and thought surrendered themselves to God, are much too hasty in their judgement. They have done something, indeed, but not at all the most difficult part of their duty, which is to surrender themselves to God in deed and act. They have as yet done nothing to show they will not, after saying 'I go', the next moment 'go not'; nothing to show they will not act the part of the self-deceiving disciple, who said, 'Though I die with Thee, I will not deny Thee', yet straightway went and denied Christ thrice.

As far as we know any thing of the matter, justifying faith has no existence independent of its particular definite acts. It may be described to be the temper under which men obey; the humble and earnest desire to please Christ which causes and attends on actual services. He who does one little deed of obedience, whether he denies himself some comfort to relieve the sick and needy, or curbs his temper, or forgives an enemy, or asks forgiveness for an offence committed by him, or resists the clamour or ridicule of the world – such an one (as far as we are given to judge) evinces more true faith than could be shown by the most fluent religious conversation, the most intimate knowledge of Scripture doctrine, or the most remarkable agitation and change of religious sentiments. Yet how many are there who sit still with folded hands, dreaming, doing nothing at all, thinking they have done every thing, or need do nothing, when they merely have had these good *thoughts*, which will save no one.

My object has been, as far as a few words can do it, to lead you to some true notion of the depths and deceitfulness of the heart, which we do not really know . . .

★   ★   ★

There has been but One amongst the sons of men who has said and done *consistently*; who said, 'I come to do Thy will, O God', and without delay or hindrance did it. He came to show us what human nature might become, if carried on to its perfection. Thus He teaches us to think highly of our nature as viewed in Him; not (as some do) to speak evil of our nature and exalt ourselves personally, but while we acknowledge *our own* distance from heaven, to view our *nature* as renewed in Him, as glorious and wonderful beyond our thoughts. Thus He teaches us to be hopeful; and encourages us while conscience abases us. Angels seem little in honour and dignity, compared with that nature which the Eternal Word has purified by His own union with it. Henceforth, we dare aspire to enter into the heaven of heavens, and to live for ever in God's presence, because the first-fruits of our race is already there in the Person of His Only-begotten Son.

The Blessed Sacrament

On the cross thy godhead made no sign to men,
Here thy very manhood steals from human ken:
Both are my confession, both are my belief,
And I pray the prayer of the dying thief.

I am not like Thomas, wounds I cannot see,
But can plainly call thee Lord and God as he;
Let me to a deeper faith daily nearer move,
Daily make me harder hope and dearer love.

O thou our reminder of Christ crucified,
Living Bread, the life of us for whom he died,
Lend this life to me then: feed and feast my mind,
There be thou the sweetness man was meant to find.

Gerard Manley Hopkins (1844–1889)
From his translation of the 'Adoro te devote'. The nineteenth century saw
many ancient prayers and hymns freshly translated for use in church.

SERMON SEVENTEEN

Charles Spurgeon

Charles Spurgeon (1834–1892) was called by a biographer an 'Heir to the Puritans'. That places his kind of Christianity, for he was a convinced Calvinist, an admirer of Bunyan and Jonathan Edwards, but it is hard to do justice to his relentlessly energetic pursuit of the ministry of preaching. A sermon by Spurgeon was published every week between August 1854 and May 1917, and they sold, it is said, 100 million at a penny each. The collected sermons fill 67 fat volumes. Thousands heard his Sunday sermons; the Metropolitan Tabernacle in London was built to accommodate his congregations of 6,000 all seated at once. He aimed to be an expositor of Scripture, preaching on every book of the Bible. He did not eschew strange titles for his sermons such as 'Am I a sea or a whale?' or 'The Shankbone Sermon'. In 1887 he withdrew from the Baptist Union over what he saw as its increasing liberalism.

No room for Christ in the inn

A sermon delivered on Sunday morning, 21 December 1862, at the Metropolitan Tabernacle, Newington.

And she brought forth her firstborn son, and wrapped him in swaddling clothes, and laid him in a manger; because there was no room for them in the inn. (Luke 2:7)

It was needful that it should be distinctly proven, beyond all dispute, that our Lord sprang out of Judah. It was necessary, also, that he should be born in Bethlehem-Ephratah, according to the word of the Lord which he spake by his servant Micah. But how could a public recognition of the lineage of an obscure carpenter and an unknown maiden be procured? What interest could the keepers of the registers be supposed to take in two such humble persons?

As for the second matter, Mary lived at Nazareth in Galilee, and there seemed every probability that the birth would take place there; indeed, the period of her delivery was so near that, unless absolutely compelled, she would not be likely to undertake a long and tedious journey to the southern province of Judea. How are these two matters to be arranged? Can one turn of the wheel effect two purposes? It can be done! It shall be done!

The official stamp of the Roman empire shall be affixed to the pedigree of the coming Son of David, and Bethlehem shall behold his nativity. A little tyrant, Herod, by some show of independent spirit, offends the greater tyrant, Augustus. Augustus informs him that he shall no longer treat him as a friend, but as a vassal; and albeit Herod makes the most abject submission, and his friends at the Roman court intercede for him, yet Augustus, to show his displeasure, orders a census to be taken of all the Jewish people, in readiness for a contemplated taxation which, however, was not carried out till some ten years after.

Even the winds and waves are not more fickle than a tyrant's will; but the Ruler of tempests knoweth how to rule the perverse spirits of princes. The Lord our God has a bit for the wildest war horse, and a hook for the most terrible leviathan. Autocratical Caesars are but puppets moved with invisible strings, mere drudges to the King of kings. Augustus must be made offended with Herod; he is constrained to tax the people; it is imperative that a census be taken; nay, it is of necessity that inconvenient, harsh, and tyrannical regulations should be published, and every person must repair to the town to which he was reputed to belong; thus, Mary is brought to Bethlehem, Jesus Christ is born as appointed, and, moreover, he is recognized officially as being descended from David by the fact that his mother came to Bethlehem as being of that lineage, remained there, and returned to Galilee without having her claims questioned, although the jealousy of all the women of the clan would have been aroused had an intruder ventured to claim a place among the few females to whom the birth of Messias was now by express prophecies confined. Remark here the wisdom of a God of providence, and believe that all things are ordered well.

When all persons of the house of David were thus driven to Bethlehem, the scanty accommodation of the little town would soon be exhausted. Doubtless friends entertained their friends till their houses were all full, but Joseph had no such willing kinsmen in the town. There was the caravanserai, which was provided in every village, where free accommodation was given to travellers; this, too, was full, for coming from a distance, and compelled to travel slowly, the humble couple had arrived late in the day. The rooms within the great brick square were already occupied with families; there remained no better lodging, even for a woman in travail, than one of the meaner spaces appropriated to beasts of burden. The stall of the ass was the only place where the child could be born. By hanging a curtain at its front, and perhaps tethering the animal on the outer side to block the passage, the needed seclusion could be obtained, and here, in the stable, was the King of Glory born, and in the manger was he laid.

My business this morning is to lead your meditations to the stable at Bethlehem, that you may see this great sight – the Saviour in the manger, and think over the reason for this lowly couch – 'because there was no room for them in the inn'.

★   ★   ★

I shall commence by remarking that there were other reasons why Christ should be laid in the manger.

First: I think it was intended thus *to show forth his humiliation*. He came, according to prophecy, to be 'despised and rejected of men, a man of sorrows and acquainted with grief'; he was to be 'without form or comeliness', 'a root out of a dry ground'. Would it have been fitting that the man who was to die naked on the cross should be robed in purple at his birth? Would it not have been inappropriate that the Redeemer who was to be buried in a borrowed tomb should be born anywhere but in the humblest shed, and housed anywhere but in the most ignoble manner?

The manger and the cross standing at the two extremities of the Saviour's earthly life seem most fit and congruous the one to the other. He is to wear through life a peasant's garb; he is to associate with fishermen; the lowly are to be his disciples; the cold mountains are often to be his only bed: he is to say, 'Foxes have holes, and the birds of the air have nests, but the Son of Man hath not where to lay his head'; nothing, therefore, could be more fitting than that in his season of humiliation, when he laid aside all his glory, and took upon himself the form of a servant, and condescended even to the meanest estate, he should be laid in a manger.

Second: By being in a manger *he was declared to be the king of the poor.* They, doubtless, were at once able to recognize his relationship to them, from the position in which they found him. I believe it excited feelings of the tenderest brotherly kindness in the minds of the shepherds, when the angel said: 'This shall be a sign unto you; you shall find the child wrapped in swaddling-clothes and lying in a manger.' In the eyes of the poor, imperial robes excite no affection, but a man in their own garb attracts their confidence. With what pertinacity will working men cleave to a leader of their own order, believing in him because he knows their toils, sympathizes in their sorrows, and feels an interest in all their concerns. Great commanders have readily won the hearts of their soldiers by sharing their hardships and roughing it as if they belonged to the ranks. The King of Men who was born in Bethlehem, was not exempted in his infancy from the common calamities of the poor, nay, his lot was even worse than theirs.

I think I hear the shepherds comment on the manger-birth. 'Ah!' said one to his fellow, 'then he will not be like Herod the tyrant; he will remember the manger and feel for the poor; poor helpless infant, I feel a love for him even now, what miserable accommodation this cold world yields its Saviour; it is not a Caesar that is born to-day; he will never trample down our fields with his armies, or slaughter our flocks for his courtiers, he will be the poor man's friend, the people's monarch; according to the words of our shepherd-king he shall judge the poor of the people; he shall save the children of the needy.'

Surely the shepherds, and such as they – the poor of the earth, perceived at once that there was the plebeian king; noble in descent, but still as the Lord hath called him, 'one chosen out of the people'. Great Prince of Peace! the manger was thy royal cradle! Therein wast thou presented to all nations as Prince of our race, before whose presence there is neither barbarian, Scythian, bond nor free; but thou art Lord of all. Kings, your gold and silver would have been lavished on him if ye had known the Lord of Glory, but inasmuch as ye knew him not he was declared with demonstration to be a leader and a witness to the people. The things which are not, under him shall bring to nought the things that are, and the things that are despised which God hath chosen, shall under his leadership break in pieces the might, and pride, and majesty of human grandeur.

Third: Further, in thus being laid in a manger, he did, as it were, *give an invitation to the most humble to come to him.* We might tremble to approach a throne, but we cannot fear to approach a manger. Had we seen the Master at first riding in state through the streets of Jerusalem with garments laid in the way, and the palm-branches strewed, and the people crying, 'Hosanna!' we might have thought, though even the thought would have been wrong, that he was not approachable. Even there, riding upon a colt the foal of an ass, he was so meek and lowly, that young children clustered about him with their boyish 'Hosanna!'

Never could there be a being more approachable than Christ. No rough guards pushed poor petitioners away; no array of officious friends were allowed to keep off the importunate widow or the man who clamoured that his son might be made whole; the hem of his garment was always trailing where sick folk could reach it, and he himself had a hand always ready to touch the disease, an ear to catch the faintest accents of misery, a soul going forth everywhere in rays of mercy, even as the light of the sun streams on every side beyond that orb itself. By being laid in a manger he proved himself a priest taken from among men, one who has suffered like his brethren, and therefore can be touched with a feeling of our infirmities.

Of him it was said: 'He doth eat and drink with publicans, and sinners'; 'this man receiveth sinners and eateth with them'. Even as an infant, by being laid in a manger, he was set forth as the sinner's friend. Come to him, ye that are weary and heavy-laden! Come to him, ye that are broken in spirit, ye who are bowed down in soul! Come to him, ye that despise yourselves and are despised of others! Come to him, publican and harlot! Come to him, thief and drunkard! In the manger there, he lies, unguarded from your touch and unshielded from your gaze. Bow the knee, and kiss the Son of God; accept him as your Saviour, for he puts himself into that manger that you may approach him. The throne of Solomon might awe you, but the manger of the Son of David must invite you.

Fourth: Methinks there was yet another mystery. You remember, brethren, that this place was *free to all*; it was an inn, and please to remember the inn in this case was not like our hotels, where accommodation and provision must be paid for. In the early and simple ages of the world every man considered it an honour to entertain a stranger; afterwards, as travelling became more common, many desired to shift the honour and pleasure upon their neighbours; wherefore should they engross all the dignity of hospitality? Further on still, some one person was appointed in each town and village, and was expected to entertain strangers in the name of the rest; but, as the ages grew less simple, and the pristine glow of brotherly love cooled down, the only provision made was the erection of a huge square block arranged in rooms for the travellers, and with lower stages for the beasts, and here, with a certain provision of water and in some cases chopped straw for the cattle, the traveller must make himself as comfortable as he could. He had not to purchase admittance to the caravanserai, for it was free to all, and the stable especially so. Now, beloved, our Lord Jesus Christ was born in the stable of the inn to show how free he is to all comers. The Gospel is preached to every creature and shuts out none. We may say of the invitations of Holy Scripture,

> None excluded hence but those
> Who do themselves exclude;
> Welcome the learned and polite,
> The ignorant and rude.
> Though Jesus' grace can save the prince,
> The poor may take their share;
> No mortal has a just pretence
> To perish in despair.

Class exclusions are unknown here, and the prerogatives of caste are not acknowledged. No forms of etiquette are required in entering a stable; it cannot be an offence to enter the stable of a public caravanserai. So, if you desire to come to Christ you may come to him just as you are; you may come *now*. Whosoever among you hath the desire in his heart to trust Christ is free to do it. Jesus is free to you; he will receive you; he will welcome you with gladness, and to show this, I think, the young child was cradled in a manger. We know that sinners often imagine that they are shut out. Oftentimes the convicted conscience will write bitter things against itself and deny its part and lot in mercy's stores.

Brother, if *God* hath not shut thee out, do not shut thyself out. Until thou canst find it written in the Book that thou mayest not trust Christ; till thou canst quote a positive passage in which it is written that he is not able to save thee, I pray thee take that other word wherein it is written – 'He is able to save unto the uttermost them that come unto God by him.' Venture on that promise: come to Christ in the strength and faith of it, and thou shalt find him free to all comers . . .

Mary

Blessed is she that hath believed, for there shall be a performance of those things which were told her from the Lord; and blessed are we, that they have been performed, if we, sinful children of the twentieth century, dare to join our voices with all generations in calling her blessed. So may she intercede for us, so may Jesus pity us, so may the Father himself pardon us, and grant us perseverance in his grace; that we, at the last, may be taken up, whither Mary has been taken up before us, through death's gates into the city of eternal peace.

Ronald Knox (1888–1957)
From 'Mary in the Thirty-Nine Articles' (1917)

Martin Luther King

Martin Luther King (1929–1968) applied the theme of liberation in the Bible to the unjust plight of black people in particular in the America of his day. He did not want to wait until the next life to see these injustices righted. Born in Atlanta, Georgia, the son of a Baptist pastor, he studied at Boston University and became a leader of the Civil Rights Movement. His extraordinary oratorical skills, matched to audiences which knew how to make the most of them, brought him success in his challenges to the segregation laws of the South. He enjoined passive resistance of a Gandhian kind, and was awarded the Nobel Prize for Peace in 1964. He was shot dead by an assassin at Memphis, Tennessee.

This sermon was delivered in the Episcopalian Cathedral of St John the Divine in New York on 17 May 1956 as part of an ecumenical programme marking the second anniversary of the desegregation decision by the Supreme Court in Brown v. Board of Education.

And Israel saw the Egyptians dead upon the seashore. (Exodus 14:30)

There is hardly anything more obvious than the fact that evil is present in the universe. It projects its nagging, prehensile tentacles into every level of human existence. We may debate over the origin of evil, but only the person victimized with a superficial optimism will debate over its reality. Evil is with us as a stark, grim, and colossal reality.

The Bible affirms the reality of evil in glaring terms. It symbolically pictures it in the work of a serpent which comes to inject a discord into the beautiful, harmonious symphony of life in a garden. It sees it in nagging tares disrupting the orderly growth of stately wheat. It sees it in a ruthless mob hanging the world's most precious character on a cross between two thieves. The Bible is crystal clear in its perception of evil.

But we need not stop with the glaring examples of the Bible to establish the reality of evil; we need only to look out into the wide arena of everyday life. We have seen evil in tragic lust and inordinate selfishness. We have seen it in high places where men are willing to sacrifice truth on the altars of their self-interest. We have seen it in imperialistic nations trampling over other nations with the iron feet of oppression. We have seen it clothed in the garments of calamitous wars which left battlefields painted with blood, filled nations with widows and orphans, and sent men home physically handicapped and psychologically wrecked. We have seen evil in all of its tragic dimensions.

So in a sense, the whole history of life is the history of a struggle between good and evil. There seems to be a tension at the very core of the universe. All the great religions have seen this tension at the centre of life. Hinduism called it a conflict between illusion and reality; Zoroastrianism looked upon it as a tension between the god of light and the god of darkness; Platonism called it a conflict between spirit and matter; traditional Judaism and Christianity called it a conflict between God and Satan. Each of these religions recognized that in the midst of the upward climb of goodness there is the down pull of evil.

The Hebraic Christian tradition is clear, however, in affirming that in the long struggle between good and evil, good eventually emerges as the victor. Evil is ultimately doomed by the powerful, insurgent forces of good. Good Friday may occupy the throne for a day, but ultimately it must give way to the triumphant beat of the drums of Easter. A mythical Satan, through the work of a conniving serpent, may gain the allegiance of man for a period, but ultimately he must give way to the magnetic redemptive power of a humble servant on an uplifted cross. Evil may so shape events that Caesar will occupy a palace and Christ a cross, but one day that same Christ will rise up and split history into AD and BC, so that even the life of Caesar must be dated by his name. Biblical religion recognized long ago what William Cullen Bryant came to see in the modern world: 'Truth crushed to earth will rise again': and what Carlyle came to see: 'No lie can live for ever.'

A graphic example of this truth is found in an incident in the early history of the Hebrew people. You will remember that at a very early stage in her history the children of Israel were reduced to the bondage of physical slavery under the gripping yoke of Egyptian rule. Egypt was the symbol of evil in the form of humiliating oppression, ungodly exploitation and crushing domination. The Israelites symbolized goodness, in the form of devotion and dedication to the God of Abraham, Isaac and Jacob. These two forces were in a continual struggle against each other – Egypt struggling to maintain her oppressive yoke and Israel struggling to gain freedom from this yoke. Finally, however, these Israelites, through the providence of God, were able to cross the Red Sea, and thereby get out of the hands of Egyptian rule. The Egyptians, in a desperate attempt to prevent the Israelites from escaping, had their armies to go in the Red Sea behind them. But as soon as the Egyptians got into the Red Sea the parted waves swept back upon them, and the rushing waters of the sea soon drowned all of them. As the Israelites looked back all they could see was here and there a poor drowned body beaten upon the seashore. For the Israelites, this was a great moment. It was the end of a frightful period in their history. It was a joyous daybreak that had come to end the long night of their captivity.

This story symbolizes something basic about the universe. It symbolizes something much deeper than the drowning of a few men, for no one can rejoice at the death or the defeat of a human person. This story, at bottom, symbolizes the death of evil. It was the death of inhuman oppression and ungodly exploitation.

The death of the Egyptians upon the seashore is a glaring symbol of the ultimate doom of evil in its struggle with good. There is something in the very nature of the universe which is on the side of Israel in its struggle with every Egypt. There is something in the very nature of the universe which ultimately comes to the aid of goodness in its perennial struggle with evil. There is something in this universe which justifies James Russell Lowell in saying:

> Truth forever on the scaffold,
> Wrong forever on the throne.
> Yet that scaffold sways the future,
> And behind the dim unknown
> Stands God within the shadow,
> Keeping watch above His own.

Notice how we have seen the truth of this text revealed in the contemporary struggle between good, in the form of freedom and justice, and evil, in the form of oppression and colonialism. Gradually we have seen the forces of freedom and justice emerge victoriously out of some Red Sea, only to look back and see the forces of oppression and colonialism dead upon the seashore.

There are approximately 2,400,000,000 people in the world today. The vast majority of these people are found in Africa and Asia. More than 1,4000,000,000 of the peoples of the world are found on these two continents. Fifty years ago most of these people were dominated politically, exploited economically, seg-regated and humiliated by some foreign power. There were 400,000,000 persons in India and Pakistan under the iron feet of British rule. There were 600,000,000 persons in China under the gripping yoke of British, Dutch and French rule. There were 100,000,000 persons in Indonesia under the oppressive hands of Dutch rule. There were 200,000,000 persons in Africa dominated and exploited by the British, the Belgians, the French, and the Dutch. The great struggle for the twentieth century has been between these exploited masses questing for freedom and the colonial powers seeking to maintain their domination.

What we are seeing now in this struggle is the gradual victory of the forces of freedom and justice. The Red Sea has opened, and today most of these exploited masses have won their freedom from the Egypt of colonialism and are now free to move toward the promised land of economic security and cultural develop-ment. As they look back they clearly see the evils of colonialism and imperialists dead upon the seashore.

In our own struggle for freedom and justice in this country we have gradually seen the death of evil. Many years ago the Negro was thrown into the Egypt of segregation and his great struggle has been to free himself from the crippling restrictions and paralysing effects of this vicious system. For years it looked like he would never get out of this Egypt. The closed Red Sea always stood before him with discouraging dimensions – there were always those Pharaohs with hardened hearts, who, despite the

175

cries of many a Moses, refused to let these people go. But one day, through a world-shaking decree by the nine justices of the Supreme Court of America and an awakened moral conscience of many white persons of goodwill, backed up by the Providence of God, the Red Sea was opened and the forces of justice marched through to the other side. As we look back we see segregation caught in the rushing waters of historical necessity. Evil in the form of injustice and exploitation cannot survive. There is a Red Sea in history that ultimately comes to carry the forces of goodness to victory, and that same Red Sea closes in to bring doom and destruction to the forces of evil.

This is our hope. This is the hope and conviction that all men of goodwill live by. It is at bottom the conviction that all reality hinges on moral foundations and that the whole cosmic universe has spiritual control. It is therefore fitting and proper that we assemble here, just two years after the Supreme Court's momentous decision on desegregation, and praise God for His power and the greatness of His purpose, and pray that we gain the vision and the will to be His co-workers in this struggle.

Let us not despair. Let us not lose faith in man and certainly not in God. We must believe that a prejudiced mind can be changed, and that man, by the grace of God, can be lifted from the valley of hate to the high mountain of love.

Let us remember that as we struggle against Egypt, we must have love, compassion and understanding goodwill for those against whom we struggle, helping them to realize that as we seek to defeat the evils of Egypt we are not seeking to defeat them but to help them, as well as ourselves.

God has a great plan for this world. His purpose is to achieve a world where all men will live together as brothers, and where every man recognizes the dignity and worth of all human personality. He is seeking at every moment of His existence to lift men from the bondage of some evil Egypt, carrying them through the wilderness of discipline, and finally to the Promised Land of personal and social integration. May it not be that this is entirely within the realm of possibility? I prefer to live by the faith that the

kingdoms of this world shall become the kingdoms of our Lord
and His Christ, and He shall reign for ever and ever.

Hallelujah!
Hallelujah!

Jesus

Jesus is
the Word – to be spoken
the Bread of life – to be eaten
the Hungry – to be fed
and the Thirsty – to be satiated.

Mother Teresa of Calcutta (1910–1997)

SERMON NINETEEN

H. A. Williams

The honesty that Harry Williams (born 1919) brought to preaching attracted a new generation who had been put off the claims of Christianity by the unexamined presuppositions of less open preachers. To get a seat at one of his sermons, Cambridge undergraduates lined up all round Great Court at Trinity College, where he was a fellow from 1951 to 1969. He had already found it impossible during parish work to retail the prevailing rules of the Church of England on sexual practice; at Cambridge he had a shattering nervous breakdown after which his idea of God was remade. He sought the true God within him. Williams lays stress on the need to lay aside pretence in belief or behaviour. He announced his own homosexuality at a time when many still saw such behaviour as a crime; he asserted that he had found true expression of love in such a relationship. In 1969, aged 50, he resigned his Fellowship at Trinity to join the Community of the Resurrection at Mirfield, West Yorkshire.

God is charity

A fundamental Christian assertion is that God is charity. There is also a well-known phrase, 'As cold as charity.' Now of course, in that phrase charity does not mean love. It means the mechanical administration of alms-giving. You put in the plate ten shillings you can well afford, and you don't have to be mixed up with the irritating human beings your money is going to help. Needless to say, nobody imagines that God's charity is like that.

But I think we can, none the less, still use the phrase, 'as cold as charity' – 'as cold as the divine charity', 'as cold as God's love'. I don't mean that God's love is in fact cold. It's much too hot for most of us most of the time. But it is often made to appear cold by those who are afraid of its heat and are on the look-out for respectable reasons for cooling it down. Thus, for instance, we are often told that God's love is totally different from natural love. The warmth, the thrill, the vital peace, of satisfactory natural love have nothing in common with true love for God, let alone God's attitude to us. Our love for God is a matter of will-power, not of anything we know as love at all. And as for God's attitude to us, it's cold and austere.

At Cana of Galilee Jesus turned water into wine. Most of us Christians spend a great deal of our time trying to turn wine into water. With regard to much human feeling, we attempt to damp it down, and if we succeed we call this negative result goodness. And we think that God is pleased, for most of us, somewhere in our heart, keep an idol of a cold-austere schoolmaster of a God. That is the chief reason, perhaps the only reason, why we sin. We deeply resent having this inhuman monster as Lord over us. To thumb-nose and kick Him is our secret pleasure, secret, very often, even from ourselves. Sometimes it breaks out into the open – especially in undergraduate magazines or television programmes, where there appears something which is openly blasphemous. But what it blasphemes against is the idol, not the true God, so the blasphemy is really a worship of the true by a making fun of the false. For when you think of a working-class woman having a baby in what are virtually slum conditions, or if you think of a man without a home, who in the end was unjustly condemned to the gallows by church people, there is nothing to sneer at or to thumb-nose. And that is the true God we worship, the God of Bethlehem, and of Calvary.

God's coming to us in the humanity of Jesus shows that His charity is the most human thing conceivable, warm, sweet, tender, as the hymn has it. That is because being human is not a shabby thing to be ashamed of. For us human beings being human is God's gift of Himself, the way in which His charity operates. Our being human is God increasing joy.

Go into a Lyons teashop with a friend. As you eat your bun together and drink your coffee, surrounded by a crowd of people, Lyons is Emmaus. Christ is present in this breaking of the bread. His love envelops you. He can make Himself known to you without your being explicitly aware of it. All you may feel is the warmth of companionship. But, when you come to think about it later, your happiness showed that Christ was there. Do you know John Betjeman's poem, 'In a Bath Teashop'?

'Let us not speak, for the love we bear one another –
Let us hold hands and look.'
She, such a very ordinary little woman;
He, such a thumping crook;
But both, for a moment, little lower than the angels
In the teashop's ingle-nook.

That is the divine charity.

Somebody in London said to me the other day that he disliked the Holy Communion because it was too personal. Lucky man. He was an accountant, so he hadn't the theological *savoir-faire* to explain away his phobia by respectable academic arguments about the nature of Godhead. He just admitted he was afraid of being a person. I know what he meant. Personal encounter of any kind can be terrifying. That is why people want to depersonalize God's love and play it cool. Otherwise, it is felt to be too threatening. The conventions of polite society, social etiquette and so forth, are a device to protect people from the onslaught of personal encounter. I can't play this game properly, but I've seen it played with exquisite skill and grace, so that people in a room together never meet each other at all. I think that quite a lot of the religious programmes and rules we adopt are parallel to social etiquette. They help us not to meet the personal, human charity of God. We escape from the real world, where we meet God's charity in what we are and in what other people are, escape into an alternative, less threatening world, called religion and church.

Why do we fear personal encounter? Well, I think it is this: it is true of practically all of us that somewhere, sometime – and almost certainly we've forgotten it – somewhere, sometime, our intrinsic tenderness has been violated. For us, therefore, encounter spells violation. A poet reads his most sacred secrets to an audience which laughs and jeers. A lover tells of his deepest feelings to be scoffed at and condemned. A child lifts up his face to be kissed and hugged, and is told to go back into the nursery. An infant stretches out its hands to its universe (its mother) to be repelled. Once bitten, twice shy. If personal encounter means such violation of tenderness, then the pain is too great, the cost too high. Let us see it doesn't happen again. Let us depersonalize ourselves so as to avoid the agony of personal encounter.

Now God's Charity won't let you stick there. He has created me to be a person, and He will carry on His work. His aim is to make me capable of the happiness He planned to give me before the foundation of the world. But to do it He must lead me to open my wounds so that He can heal them. And this opening of wounds is always painful. Perhaps we may put it thus: God has created the whole of what I am, so He won't allow me to keep part of myself anaesthetized. He wakes up what I would keep asleep, and the result is inner conflict. This terrible concern of God for the whole of me is what I believe is meant by His wrath. He won't let sleeping dogs lie because He knows that I can't be truly happy unless and until I am fully myself. When I have learnt to receive what I would now refuse, then there will be no more conflict. But it takes time, probably a lifetime. This is what I have called the opening of wounds. God does it for us by means of our ordinary experience of life – by our succeeding, working, failing, falling in love, getting into a stew, feeling angry – the whole kaleidoscope of living. And when this is happening it feels as though God isn't there. His charity seems an illusion. If God cared, how could He let us endure such things and be reduced to such a state? What is hidden from it is God's concern that nothing we are should be lost. Here I want to quote some remarkable words of Proust. 'When,' says Proust, 'in the course of my life, I have had occasion to meet with, in convents, for instance, literally saintly examples of practical charity, they have generally had the brisk, decided, undisturbed, and slightly brutal air of a busy surgeon, the face in which one can discern no commiseration, no tenderness at the sight of suffering humanity and no fear of hurting it, the face devoid of gentleness or sympathy, the sublime face of true goodness.'

That is how God's love can feel like when He is opening our wounds to heal them. Like a great surgeon, He has no fear of hurting us because of His absolute competence to make us well.

The knife is securely in His hands. In the operating theatre, the surgeon's face only *looks* devoid of gentleness of sympathy, for his whole work, his entire commitment and vocation, flows from his desire to help and to heal. And there can be no deeper sympathy than that, no more effective gentleness. The God we worship has shown forth His sympathy and gentleness, His Charity, by being wounded Himself in order the better to heal us –

> The wounded surgeon plies the steel
> That questions the distempered part;
> Beneath the bleeding hands we feel
> The sharp compassion of the healer's art
> Resolving the enigma of the fever chart.

So we must not be taken in when it feels as if God doesn't care. For in fact He is allowing us to be turned inside out and shaken upside down in order to give us the openness to life, the ability to receive life without fear, which belongs to a full person. We must not worry about it with fretful scheming. We must trust God to do it for us because He is Charity. The world is charged with the grandeur of God. It will flame out. Because the Holy Ghost over the bent world broods with warm breast. Our world, the world which is us – all we are and do and suffer. There is charity flaming out, creating us. For God's charity is not a sort of wireless wave or spiritual chemical. It comes to us incarnated, inseparably bound up with our whole human experience. It is by means of our living our human lives in this world that God is creating us.

But if charity is thus to create you, you mustn't protect yourself from it behind the shelter of the preconceived idea. What I mean is you mustn't start with the assumption that charity must always involve a certain set of particular actions, or must never involve another set of particular actions. For in this case charity ceases to be itself and becomes the slave of a culture.

Sixty years ago many of the upper and middle classes sincerely believed that charity involved never going on strike. Today, the Roman Catholic Church still believes that true charity between husband and wife forbids the practice of contraception. Be careful of the commands and prohibitions which are said to protect charity, for such protection sometimes turns out in fact to be protective custody, because charity threatens the vested interests of the *status quo*. If you want the point further elucidated, read the works of the Catholic novelist, Graham Greene. Few people in our time have understood so profoundly or set out so illuminatingly what it means to resist charity or to be created by it.

Another thing to remember is that charity is God's giving His 'isness' to you. In consequence you find yourself the sort of person who really loves other people instead of the sort of person who tries to act as though he did. When people say that I acted charitably towards so and so, what they generally mean is that in fact I hate his guts but managed to behave as though I didn't. This use of the word in common parlance is a sign of disbelief in God's ability really to change me, as if to say that He can't alter me fundamentally, but only supply me with a sort of spiritual benzedrine which enables me to perform feats beyond my natural condition. 'Charity tries to suffer long, charity tries to be kind, it tries not to envy, it tries to be not easily provoked. Charity tries to bear all things, tries to believe all things, tries to hope all things, tries to endure all things.' That is how in our mind we re-write St Paul's great chapter. But charity doesn't try. It is, because God is. That is the miracle to belief in which all Christians everywhere are fundamentally committed – the miracle of our becoming like God by sharing His life.

Now what I have just said is often confused with something very different, namely, that we should always give way to the impulse of the moment. But nobody could live at all in society if they did this. Discipline and self-control are essential. But they are of two kinds and spring from two sources. In the words of Jesus, one kind imposes heavy burdens, grievous to be borne, and lays them upon men's shoulders. The other kind is described in the words, 'My yoke is easy, and my burden is light.'

Suppose, for example, that I came from a family of competent scientists, and my father expected me to carry on the family tradition. As it happens, my real interests are in literature, not science. But in loyalty to my family and in obedience to my father's wishes I go slogging away preparing for the Natural Sciences Tripos. I discipline myself to do ten hours work a day. But I don't make any progress and the discipline is making me depressed and on edge. In the end it becomes too much for me to bear and I leave Cambridge. My work has been one long denial of what I really am, for my real interests are literary. But suppose, on the contrary, that I was studying for the English Tripos. My work would still require effort, discipline, and self-control. For to go to the cinema or the pub would often seem more immediately inviting than studying Milton. Yet because of my literary interests and abilities, the discipline I impose upon myself is not a perpetual denial of what I am but a perpetual affirmation of it. So, although I do a great deal of work, I am profoundly happy and grow in stature as a person. Charity's discipline is of this second kind. It is a constant self-affirmation, like a pianist devoted to his art, who will do anything, however laborious, and give up anything, however attractive, in order to perfect his technique, and thereby find his life. Once we are certain that a discipline enables us to be ourselves, to share God's isness, the yoke will be easy and the burden light, whatever it entails.

The Christian gospel is the assertion that God creates us the sort of people to whom Charity is natural, a self-affirmation. Jesus, we are told, for the joy that was set before Him, endured the Cross – charity at its completest and most absolute. And Jesus gives His Spirit to us – or so, at least, we claim to believe.

> The Angel that presided o'er my birth
> Said 'Little creature, form'd of joy and mirth,
> Go, love without the help of anything on earth.'

Extract from a sermon by Billy Graham,
California, 1974

There came one runing, and kneeled to him, and asked him,
Good Master, what shall I do that I may inherit eternal life?
(Mark 10:17)

Now there are many things I would like to say about this passage
tonight. It's the story of a young aristocrat coming to Jesus Christ.
Handsome, we can suppose, certainly wealthy and young, but he
was like thousands of young people and older people alike here
tonight. He was seeking something else in life. He wasn't satisfied
with the way life was at the moment. The pressures of life were
too great. He might have been a university student, he might have
been a senior student, I don't know. But right now we have a
phenomenon that's been sweeping America for about eight or
ten years. Younger people have suddenly become interested in
religion, once again.

Now as I look on young people today I want to give you
eleven things that I see among young people, and I'm old enough
to say 'you young people'. I'm 56 years of age if you want to
know my age. I have five children and nine grandchildren and
two on the way. So tonight I want you to see yourselves the way I
see you.

First, I believe there is a breakdown of home life, and it has led
to moral and spiritual void. Even in some of the finest Christian
homes, the God has become television. That little set we gather
around – the only time the family is quiet, the only time the family
has any little reverence is around that set. It used to be around the
family Bible, it used to be around God, it used to be around prayer
but now about the only time you can get the family together is if
they agree on a certain programme, and if they don't, most homes
now have two sets so you divide the family. But there is a spiritual
void, and when you think of one out of every two or three
marriages breaking up, you have millions of young people being

thrown out without the roots of a father and mother at home; and then in the homes that stay together, you have a lack of love between parents many times, and the young people feel this and they are affected psychologically and spiritually.

Second, I find a tremendous dissatisfaction among young people with their lives as they are. A young person told me just the other day, 'I don't know what's wrong. I've got everything. I am a senior at the university but', he said, 'I'm just dissatisfied with myself.' I said, 'Do you know why?' I said, 'Everybody has this same type of dissatisfaction until they find it in Jesus Christ.'

And then, third, I find in this generation of young people that sexual relationships don't provide the emotional closeness they thought they would. They are not finding the peace and happiness and the kicks and the deep satisfaction they thought they would find in all the so-called sex freedom. It has brought about a whole new set of psychological problems that affect them the rest of their lives, especially their future marriage.

And then, fourth, I find tremendous loneliness among young people. They can have friends, they can be in a crowd but there is also loneliness. You know why. You're lonely for God. You were made for God. You were made in God's image and you are lonely for him and don't know it.

We had one of the great psychiatrists of the country here the other night, and he said to me, when he came into the little trailer, that one of the great problems he has to deal with in his great psychiatric clinic is the problem of loneliness on the part of young people. Jesus can be closer than a brother. He can settle that loneliness. You see, you were made for God, for fellowship with God, and without God there is loneliness. Give your life to Christ tonight and never know another lonely moment.

Then, fifth, I find among people, young people, restlessness. They're very restless. Now a certain amount of restlessness during a teen-age period is normal. I've had five teenage children and they were all restless. From a parent's point of view, they just had more energy than we had – that was really the problem.

Sixth, there's another kind of deeper restlessness that I'm

talking about. I'm not talking about just getting up and running around and jumping around and riding a motorcycle and all these things. That comes with being a teenager. But there is a restlessness where they don't find peace and rest until they come to know Christ in a personal way.

Then, seventh, there is a feeling of emptiness and purposelessness. They haven't found purpose and meaning in their lives, so they are empty and they are bored. Let Christ come into your heart and fill that emptiness and take that boredom away.

And then, eighth, I find that many young people are despondent. They despair easily. They get discouraged, they get down in the dumps, they have depressions, and many of them are going to see psychiatrists and psychologists and clergy, trying to get something to pick them up, and a great many prescriptions today are being given to young people that need a little – pickup.

And then, ninth, I find that for this generation of young people it's almost impossible for them to make decisions. About vocation, marriage, moral values, if there is a moral code or a moral absolute to make a decision about it.

And then, tenth, I find a sense of guilt, and they don't know why. But it's there and it causes all kinds of psychological problems. Well, of course, we are guilty. We have broken God's law. There is a right kind of guilt. There is a psychological guilt that's wrong, but there's a right kind of guilt in which you are guilty before God of breaking God's law, and that's called sin and it needs to be repented of, and it needs to be brought to the cross, and then don't let the devil put that guilt back on you. When you are forgiven by God, you are forgiven, and God not only forgives, he forgets, and when you are justified in the sight of God that means just as though you have never sinned.

Come to Christ tonight. Let him take that guilt away.

Then, eleventh, I find that disillusionment is beginning to grow, and I'm delighted at this, and I hope I'm right. I read it in one of the magazines – our disillusionment with drugs as the answer to the problems that young people were using five or six or seven or eight years ago, when they thought that LSD and all the rest of it were the ultimate of experience, and now they are beginning to be educated to the fact that this is destructive . . .

Now what about you? I think that many of you are like this young man. You've been searching for something . . .

Prayer for murderers

Oh God, we remember not only Bahram, but also his murderers. Not only because they killed him in the prime of his youth and made our hearts bleed and our tears flow. Not because with this savage act they have brought further disgrace on the name of our country among the civilized nations of the world. But because through their crime, we now follow thy footsteps more closely in the way of sacrifice.

The terrible fire of this calamity burns up all selfishness and possessiveness in us. Its flame reveals the depth of depravity and meanness and suspicion, the dimension of hatred and the measure of sinfulness in human nature. It makes obvious, as never before, our need to trust God's love as shown in the Cross of Jesus and his resurrection; a love which makes us free from hate towards our persecutors.

Bishop Dehqani-Tafti of Iran, on the murder of his son Bahram, 1980

Pope John Paul II

Karol Wojtyla (born 1920) shared the sufferings of his native Poland
during the Second World War, when he had to undertake hard labour in
a quarry and a chemical factory. He studied undercover for the priesthood
in Cracow, an Archbishopric which he was later to fill. From the 1950s to
the 1970s he carried on in firm resistance to the Communist rulers of
Poland. He was given the task of recommending to his fellow bishops how
Vatican II should be implemented there. All the time he developed a
spirituality that borrowed much from the Carmelite mystics and concen-
trated on the intervention in history of Jesus as God and a human being.
In 1978 he was elected Pope with the name of John Paul; his pontificate
has had huge effects for Church and politics. In 1979 he visited Poland
for eight days during which 10 million, a third of the country saw him.
The sermon here was given in Victory Square, Warsaw, and was often
interrupted by applause. There is no doubt that Communism in Europe
fell as suddenly as it did under the impact of this man.

Beloved fellow-countrymen, dear brothers and sisters, partici-
pants in the Eucharistic Sacrifice celebrated today in Victory
Square in Warsaw,

Together with you I wish to sing a hymn of praise to Divine
Providence, which enables me to be here as a pilgrim.

We know that the recently deceased Paul VI, the first pilgrim
Pope after so many centuries, ardently desired to set foot on the
soil of Poland, especially at Jasna Gora. To the end of his life he
kept this desire in his heart, and with it he went to the grave. And
we feel that this desire – a desire so potent and so deeply rooted
that it goes beyond the span of a pontificate – is being realized
today in a way that it would have been difficult to foresee. And so
we thank Divine Providence for having given Paul VI so strong a
desire. We thank it for the pattern of the pilgrim Pope that he
began with the Second Vatican Council. At a time when the
whole Church has become newly aware of being the People of
God – a People sharing in the mission of Christ, a People that goes
through history with that mission, a 'pilgrim' People – the Pope
could no longer remain a 'prisoner of the Vatican'. He had to
become again the pilgrim Peter, like the first Peter, who from

Jerusalem, via Antioch, reached Rome to give witness there to Christ and seal his witness with his blood.

Today it is granted to me to fulfil this desire of the deceased Pope Paul VI in the midst of you, beloved sons and daughters of my motherland. When, after the death of Paul VI and the brief pontificate of my immediate predecessor John Paul I, which lasted only a few weeks, I was, through the inscrutable designs of Divine Providence, called by the votes of the Cardinals from the chair of Saint Stanislaus in Cracow to that of Saint Peter in Rome, I immediately understood that it was for me to fulfil that desire, the desire that Paul VI had been unable to carry out at the Millennium of the Baptism of Poland.

My pilgrimage to my motherland in the year in which the Church in Poland is celebrating the ninth centenary of the death of Saint Stanislaus is surely a special sign of the pilgrimage that we Poles are making down through the history of the Church not only along the ways of our motherland but also along those of Europe and the world. Leaving myself aside at this point, I must nonetheless with all of you ask myself why, precisely in 1978, after so many centuries of a well-established tradition in this field, a son of the Polish nation, of the land of Poland, was called to the chair of Saint Peter. Christ demanded of Peter and of the other Apostles that they should be his 'witnesses in Jerusalem and in all Judea and Samaria and to the end of the earth' (Acts 1:8). Have we not the right, with reference to these words of Christ, to think that Poland has become nowadays the land of a particularly responsible witness? The right to think that from here – from Warsaw, and also from Gniezno, from Jasna Gora, from Cracow and from the whole of this historic route that I have so often in my life traversed and that it is right that I should traverse it again during these days – it is necessary to proclaim Christ with singular humility but also with conviction? The right to think that one must come to this very place, to this land, on this route, to read again the witness of his Cross and his Resurrection? But if we accept all that I have dared to affirm in this moment, how many great duties and oblig- ations arise? Are we capable of them? . . .

It is good that my pilgrimage to Poland on the ninth centenary of the martyrdom of Saint Stanislaus should fall in the Pentecost period and on the solemnity of the Most Holy Trinity . . . In the apostles who receive the Holy Spirit on the day of Pentecost are spiritually present in a way all their successors, all the Bishops, including those whose task it has been for a thousand years to proclaim the Gospel on Polish soil. Among them was this Stanislaus of Szczepanow, who paid with his blood for his mission on the episcopal chair of Cracow nine centuries ago . . .

To Poland the Church brought Christ, the key to understanding that great and fundamental reality that is man. For man cannot be fully understood without Christ. Or rather, man is incapable of understanding himself fully without Christ. He cannot understand who he is, nor what his true dignity is, nor what his vocation is, nor what his final end is. He cannot understand any of this without Christ.

Therefore Christ cannot be kept out of the history of man in any part of the globe, at any longitude or latitude of geography. The exclusion of Christ from the history of man is an act against man. Without Christ it is impossible to understand the history of Poland, especially the history of the people who have passed or are passing through this land. The history of people. The history of the nation is above all the history of people. And the history of each person unfolds in Jesus Christ. In him it becomes the history of salvation. . . .

It is impossible without Christ to understand and appraise the contribution of the Polish nation to the development of man and his humanity in the past and its contribution today also: 'This old oak tree has grown in such a way and has not been knocked down by any wind since its root is Christ', as Piotr Skarga wrote. It is necessary to follow the traces of what, or rather who, Christ was for the sons and daughters of this land down the generations. Not only for those who openly believed in him and professed him with the faith of the Church, but also for those who appeared to be at a distance, outside the Church. For those who doubted or were opposed . . .

It is impossible without Christ to understand this nation with its past so full of splendour, and also of terrible difficulties. It is impossible to understand this city, Warsaw, the capital of Poland, that undertook in 1944 an unequal battle against the aggressor, a battle in which it was abandoned by the allied powers, a battle in which it was buried under its own ruins – if it is not remembered that 'under those same ruins there was also the statue of Christ the Saviour with his cross that is in front of the church at Krakowskie Przedmiescie'. It is impossible to understand the history of Poland from Stanislaus in Skalka to Maximilian Kolbe at Auschwitz unless we apply to them that same single fundamental criterion that is called Jesus Christ.

The millennium of the baptism of Poland, of which Saint Stanislaus is the first mature fruit – the millennium of Christ in our yesterday and today is the chief reason for my pilgrimage, for my prayer of thanksgiving together with all of you, dear fellow-countrymen, to whom Christ does not cease to teach the great cause to man; together with you, for whom Jesus Christ does not cease to be an ever-open book on man, his dignity and his rights and also a book of knowledge on the dignity and rights of the nation.

Today, here in Victory Square, in the capital of Poland, I am asking with all of you, through the great Eucharistic prayer, that Christ will not cease to be for us an open book of life for the future, for our Polish future.

We are before the tomb of the Unknown Soldier. In the ancient and contemporary history of Poland this tomb has a special basis, a special reason for its existence. In how many places in our native land has that soldier fallen! In how many places in Europe and the world has he cried with his death that there can be no just Europe without the independence of Poland marked on its map! On how many battlefields has that soldier given witness to the rights of man, indelibly inscribed in the inviolable rights of the people, by falling for 'our freedom and yours'!

★   ★   ★

I wish to kneel before this tomb to venerate every seed that falls into the earth and dies and thus bears fruit. It may be the seed of the blood of a soldier shed on the battlefield, or the sacrifice of matyrdom in concentration camps or in prisons. It may be the seed of hard daily toil, with the sweat of one's brow, in the fields, the workshop, the mine, the foundries and the factories. It may be the seed of the love of parents who do not refuse to give life to a new human being and undertake the whole of the task of bringing him up. It may be the seed of creative work in the universities, the higher institutes, the libraries and the places where the national culture is built. It may be the seed of prayer, of service of the sick, the suffering, the abandoned – 'all that of which Poland is made'.

All that in the hands of the Mother of God – at the foot of the cross on Calvary and in the Upper Room of Pentecost.

All that – the history of the motherland shaped for a thousand years by the succession of the generations (among them the present generation and the coming generation) and by each son and daughter of the motherland, even if they are anonymous and unknown like the soldier before whose tomb we are now.

All that – including the history of the peoples that have lived with us and among us, such as those who died in their hundreds of thousands within the walls of the Warsaw Ghetto.

All that I embrace in thought and in my heart during this Eucharist and I include it in this unique most holy Sacrifice of Christ, on Victory Square.

And I cry – I who am a Son of the land of Poland and who am also Pope John Paul II – I cry from all the depths of this Millennium, I cry on the vigil of Pentecost:

> Let your Spirit descend.
> Let your Spirit descend,
> and renew the face of the earth,
> the face of this land.
> Amen.

Sources and Further Reading

Many old sermons are best read through public libraries, for they are often out of print or very expensive in new scholarly editions.

Page 3: St Ignatius: adapted from *The Epistles of St Ignatius*, edited by J. H. Srawley (SPCK, 1900). The writings of Ignatius are also available in English in the remarkable series of Ante-Nicene, Nicene, and Post-Nicene Fathers published in the late nineteenth century and republished by T & T Clark, Edinburgh, and William B. Eerdmans, Grand Rapids, Michigan. The language is old-fashioned.

Page 5: John Chrysostom: adapted from the Nicene and Post-Nicene Fathers. There is a lively modern translation in *John Chrysostom* by Wendy Mayer and Pauline Allen (Routledge, London and New York, 2000).

Page 13: St Patrick: adapted from *St Patrick* by Newport J. D. White (SPCK, London; Macmillan, New York, 1920). The text and meaning of St Patrick's writings are vexed.

Page 15: St Augustine: adapted from Nicene and Post-Nicene Fathers. There is a lively modern translation of the sermons in the multi-volume edition of *The Works of St Augustine* (New City Press, New Rochelle, New York, 1997).

Page 18: Alcuin: this prayer was translated by Helen Waddell in her *More Latin Lyrics from Virgil to Milton*, edited by Dame Felicitas Corrigan (Victor Gollancz, London, 1976).

Page 19: Aelfric: adapted from *Aelfric's Lives of Saints* (Early English Text Society, 1900).

Page 27: St Bernard: adapted from *Cantica Canticorum: Eighty-Six Sermons on the Song of Solomon*, translated by Samuel J. Eales (Elliott Stock, London 1895). This includes an introduction by the great seventeenth-century historian Jean Mabillon.

Page 31: St Thomas Aquinas: an English translation by John M. Ashley of Aquinas's sermon notes was published in 1873 as *The Homilies of St Thomas Aquinas*, and has been reprinted by Roman Catholic Books, Fort Collins, Colorado.

Page 34: St Francis: *The Writings of St Francis of Assisi*, translated by Paschal Robinson, was published by J. M. Dent (London, 1906). For a thorough study, there is the two-volume *Saint Francis of Assisi, Omnibus of Sources*, edited by Marion A. Habig (Franciscan Press, Quincy University, 1991).

Page 35: Our Fader: this translation is put in context in Eamon Duffy's *The Stripping of the Altars* (Yale, New Haven and London, 1992).

Page 37: *The Two Books of Homilies* (Oxford, 1859).

Page 43: St Teresa of Avila: adapted from *The Complete Works of St Teresa of Jesus*, translated by E. A. Peers, three volumes (London, 1950). There is a translation in more modern English, *The Collected Works of St Teresa of Avila*, translated by Kieran Kavanaugh and Otilio Rodriguez, three volumes (Institute of Carmelite studies, Washington DC, 1985). This edition also gives the text of the poems in Spanish.

Page 45: Lancelot Andrewes: *Ninety-Six Sermons* (John Henry Parker, Oxford, 1841).

Page 57: Morning Prayer: from *Preces Privatae*, translated by F. E. Brightman (Methuen, London, 1903).

Page 59: John Donne: *LXXX Sermons* (London, 1640) is a rare book, but not much more expensive than *The Sermons of John Donne, in Ten Volumes*, edited by Evelyn M. Simpson and George R. Potter (University of California Press, 1953–1961). Extracts from the sermons may be found in *John Donne: Selected Prose*, edited by Helen Gardner and T. Healy (Oxford, 1967).

Page 78: George Herbert: the poetry is readily available in cheap or expensive editions.

Page 79: Jeremy Taylor: *The Whole Works of Jeremy Taylor in Ten Volumes*, edited by Reginald Heber (Longmans, Green and Co., London, 1883).

Page 86: The Book of Common Prayer is in print in a variety of editions. It is easy to find, and cheap, as a secondhand book.

Page 87: John Bunyan: *The Whole Works of John Bunyan*, edited by George Offor, three volumes (Blackie and Co., London, revised 1862) is a useful edition. A scholarly edition in many volumes is being produced by the Oxford University Press.

Page 95: John Gother: *The Spiritual Works of the Reverend John Gother in 16 Volumes* (London and Newcastle) was published in several eighteenth-century editions.

Page 97: Jonathan Swift: *The Prose Works of Jonathan Swift*, edited by Temple Scott, four volumes (G. Bell, London, 1910). A scholarly edition of Swift's poetry and prose is published by Oxford University Press.

Page 106: Christopher Smart: *The Collected Poems of Christopher Smart*, edited by Norman Callan, were published in two volumes by Routledge and Kegan Paul (London, 1949). Since then, the fragments of the extraordinary poem 'Jubilate Agno' have been more convincingly arranged, as in the scholarly edition from Oxford Univerity Press, 1980 onwards.

Page 109: Jonathan Edwards: *The Works of President Edwards in Eight Volumes* (James Black, London, 1817). There has been a revival of interest in Edwards, and paperback editions of his sermons are available from several publishers. A paperback selection is *The Sermons of Jonathan Edwards: A Reader*, edited by Wilson H. Kimnach, Kenneth P. Minkema and Douglas A. Sweeney (Yale, New Haven and London, 1999).

Page 125: Hester Chapone: *Posthumous Works* (London, 1807). Mrs Chapone was a friend of Samuel Johnson's. His own sermons are published as the fourteenth volume of the Yale edition of his works (New Haven and London, 1978).

Page 127: John Wesley: *The Works of John Wesley* (Wesleyan-Methodist Book-Room, London, no date, but mid-nineteenth century). Editions of Wesley's works are numerous. His letters and his journals have been published in several volumes, sometimes in 'popular' editions. Reliability is sometimes a problem; an excellent sermon entitled 'The Cause and Cure of

Earthquakes' is often printed as John Wesley's, but is now attributed to his brother Charles. Charles's hymns are printed in most wide anthologies of hymns.

Page 135: Richard Challoner: from *The Garden of the Soul* (Burns and Oates, London, 1876). First published in 1740, this prayer book defined the spirituality of a century of Roman Catholics in England. It was much adapted and added to through the years.

Page 137: Laurence Sterne: *Sermons* (London, 1787).

Page 143: Sydney Smith: *Sermons* (London, 1846). There is an excellent modern study by Alan Bell (London, 1980). *Twelve Miles from a Lemon: Selected Writings of Sydney Smith*, compiled by Norman Taylor and Alan Hankinson (Lutterworth Press, Cambridge, 1996) includes some of his thoughts on sermons.

Page 154: John Keble: his collection of poems *The Christian Year*, first published in 1827, went through 95 editions in his lifetime. Keble's own sermon on 'National Apostasy' (1834) was regarded as the start of the Oxford Movement.

Page 155: John Henry Newman: *Parochial and Plain Sermons in 8 Volumes*, a new edition (Rivingtons, London, Oxford and Cambridge). Newman slightly corrected his works in later years. His most popular works are available in paperback or secondhand. The 30 volumes of his *Letters and Diaries* (Oxford University Press) are still not fully published, although the volumes first published are now out of print.

Page 162: Gerard Manley Hopkins: the poetry is readily available in paperback and hardback.

Page 165: Charles Spurgeon: *The Metropolitan Tabernacle Pulpit, Volume 8: Sermons Preached by C. H. Spurgeon During the Year 1862* (Passmore and Alabaster, London, 1892).

Page 170: Ronald Knox: *University and Anglican Sermons*, edited by Philip Caraman (Burns and Oates, London, 1963). Knox published many books on spiritual themes, as well as a translation of the Bible, and some detective stories. His *Enthusiasm* (Oxford, 1950) is a classic study of the religion of feeling and abnormal phenomena.

Page 171: Martin Luther King: from volume 3 of *The Papers of Martin Luther King* (University of California Press, Berkeley, Los Angeles and London, 1997).

Page 177: Mother Teresa of Calcutta: *A Fruitful Branch on the Vine, Jesus*, edited by the missionaries of Charity (St Anthony Messenger Press, Cincinnati, Ohio, 1998).

Page 179: H. A. Williams: *The True Wilderness* (Mowbray, London, 1994).

Page 187: Billy Graham: this sermon is put in context in: *Graham: A Day in Billy's Life* by Gerald S. Strober (Doubleday, Garden City, New York, 1976).

Page 191: Pope John Paul II: the sermons and encyclicals are published in a large variety of editions; many are on the internet. By far the best biography is *Witness to Hope* by George Weigel (HarperCollins, London and New York, revised edition 2001).